How
to make
Today
the
Best Day
of your
LIFE

DR. MARK
VON EHRENKROOK

ISBN:1502833913
ISBN-13:9781502833914

DEDICATION

This book is lovingly dedicated to the One
who gave His life for you and me.

ACKNOWLEDGEMENTS

I gratefully acknowledge the help and encouragement I received in the publishing of this book. It would not have been possible without the support of my precious wife; Susan. She put up with all the time it took to write the manuscript, gave helpful suggestions and even designed the cover. I also want to thank the people of Jovita Baptist Church for their love and support, without which, this book could never have seen the light of day. And, to my wonderful editor and daughter: "Your grate!) Amanda!

CONTENTS

LIVING FULLY IN THE NOW

FREEDOM

SETBACKS

LIVING THE LIFE

APPENDIXES

INTRODUCTION

I wrote this book for me, to change my life. I want to change and be a positive person, and I want to be a positive influence in your life. In the pages that follow, I hope to encourage you by sharing a part of my story, and how by changing my thinking my life was changed.

In publishing this book, I seek to encourage the Church to live one day at a time. If you live as God has planned, every day is a new adventure.

The premise of this book is the conviction that today can become the best day of your life. In the pages that follow, I would like to share with you some observations and learnings I have made as a fellow traveler.

The book is arranged into four sections with six chapters under each section. At the end of each chapter are questions to help you process the material. You can choose to do a chapter a day and finish the book in one month, or you can do a chapter a week and finish in six months. Whatever you choose to do, I am sure working through the questions at the end of each chapter will be very helpful.

The chapters are meant to stand alone, but they do relate to one of the four sections. An appendix of axioms and proverbs is located at the end of the book. These are nuggets of truth that should be committed to memory.

Remember, the decision to make this day the best day of your life must be accompanied by the doing. This book will help guide you into the action steps that will empower you to make significant changes in your life. It will help you shape your thinking. So put your mind into it, let these concepts take shape in you, and you will soon find that today really is, the best day of your life.

You do not have to be content with a life that is mostly dull and only occasionally broken by the memory of some great days of the past. Each day can be the best day ever for you, if you will follow some of the guidelines this book and change your thinking. If you change how you think, you will change how you live. It really is that simple.

Are you open to living the life God intends for you? Are you willing to change your actions and attitudes to experience today, the best day of your life?

.

1.

HOW TO MAKE TODAY
THE BEST DAY OF YOUR LIFE

"This is the day the Lord has made
Let us rejoice and be glad in it."
Psalm 118:24

She is the love of my life. My wife. We met as children, and reunited as young adults. I remember those days vividly, but the day we married was by far one of the most magnificent days I ever experienced.

As a young couple, we moved to Japan, and our first son was born. What a precious day! Those of you who've experienced the birth of your own child know what I'm talking about. We had two more children, born in the States. Amazing days, priceless memories, precious children.

I'm sure you have best day memories. Those times when you feel like the world could end and you would be most contented person on earth, just being where you are, doing what you're doing. When you think of the best day you ever had, is it associated with some sort of event?

You have memories, good memories, and maybe sad memories. But, memories of events or feelings are not what life is about. Life is about living.

What if your capacity to experience life more fully, and live more deeply and joyfully, grew each day? That wouldn't take away from the memory of special days of the past; it may even add value to those treasured moments.

What if every day became your best day ever? What if today was the best day you experienced in your life, this far? How does that prospect make you feel? Does it even sound doable?

Today Can Be the Best Day of Your Life

Reasons For	Reasons Against
Each day is a new adventure to explore.	My days are filled with "ruts."
If I change how I see my life, I can create productive actions.	Life is dull, and meaningless, with the exception of a few special memories.
Misery loves comedy—dwell on the good.	Misery loves company—dwell in the gloom.
Anticipation	Expectation
God-centered	Self-centered

Let's consider this awesome idea that today can be the best day of your life. What are the implications of that remarkable idea? One outcome would be that each day would be a mystery to be explored, not a rut to be endured. People living each day to the fullest have anticipation, and think, "I wonder what exciting thing is going to happen?" People not living life to the fullest, live with expectation, and they think, "I knew that was going to happen." We will discuss this more in length later, but it is a very important, small distinction that makes a huge difference in how you live and what life brings into your day.

Negative

I believe that negative, self-depreciating thoughts will restrain you from pursuing the life you want. Dwelling on past failures or setbacks constricts thinking and strangles lives. There seems to be in each one of us, a hindering spirit that keeps us from being "all in" every day of our lives.

Too many people live their lives in a rut, in the sameness and drudgery of the day before. The gloom and doom person will obviously find gloom and doom all around themselves in order to prove their particular mindset. This "rut" way of living is not acceptable and should not be considered normal for a functional, alive, human being.

You might argue that if today was the best day of your life, that would diminish the value or importance put on the other days that you considered the best day of your life. But would it really do that? Seriously?

Positive

An amazing outcome of living each day as the best day ever is that it really does become the best day of your life, up to now. Most people are aware of the concept of a self-fulfilling prophecy: You get what you think about, what you dwell on.

Positive people naturally have positive things come into their lives. When you live with a positive mindset, you project into you life what you want to see happen. You can live with anticipation: "I wonder what exciting thing is going to happen?!"

Committing to make today, the very best day of your life makes sense on so many levels. Why wouldn't you want every day to be better than the one before? What is keeping you from experiencing the joy and satisfaction of this anticipatory lifestyle?

Controlling Your Response

The secret to making today the best day of your life is the simple act of deciding and determining that it will be the best day of your life. You are in control of most of the factors in your life. You cannot control every detail, but you can decide how the experiences of the day will impact your life and your outlook. You are totally in charge of what you think and how you act. You have a God-given free will to decide for yourself what you will think about something and how you will respond.

You cannot control what happens to you today, but you have total control over how those experiences will impact your life.

> Look at a person like Helen Keller, blind and deaf, yet living life to the fullest and enriching lives wherever she went. Helen[1] experienced life more fully, and shared love and encouragement more broadly, than many people who take for granted their gift of sight and hearing. Helen decided that she would not let her handicap keep her from the joy of living and giving. An amazing teacher taught Helen that she

---

[1] While exploring in the National Cathedral in Washington, D.C., my wife and I came upon the crypt of Helen Keller in one of the chapels. She is interred with her dear teacher; Ann Sullivan Macy.

could not control what came into her life, but she could completely control what she did with her life.

There is an incredible latent power in you to control your destiny by controlling your thinking. This is done one day, one moment, one idea at a time.

Unfortunately, I lived much of my life reacting to circumstances instead of responding to them. I did not think about it, I just reacted emotionally. When I reacted, it was like a knee jerk reaction; the first thing that came into my mind. Later I learned to wait (count to ten, remember?), and when I waited I would think about a measured response. Not going with my first reaction, but waiting for my thoughtful response, has been very helpful.

Make the Decision

Making the decision to make today the best day of your life is the first step. If you don't take action on your ideas, you are only dreaming and will not accomplish what you set out to do. It is like the (trick) math question, "If there are five frogs on a log and one decides to jump in, how many frogs are left on the log?" The answer is five. You see, one has only *decided* to jump in, he has not committed to jumping in until he actually makes the leap. I have a plaque in my office that states, *"Knowledge isn't power until it does something."*[2] Your decision must be accompanied by your doing.

When the car won't start, or someone cuts you off on the highway, or a store clerk is discourteous with you, do you let

---

[2] Quote attributed to Dale Carnegie: "Knowledge isn't power until it is applied."

those events and people decide how you should feel and think? Many people have been conditioned to let those events and people decide whether or not today will be a good day. But the reality is that you have the power to invest in each experience exactly what you want to make it.

Ladder of Assumption

During the day your minds search out for us what you are thinking and believing about your day and yourselves. This is called the "ladder of assumption," and will be discussed in greater detail later in the book. Simply put, when you assume something to be true, your minds naturally look for proof that it is so. When you tell your minds to assume that today will be the best day ever your minds go to work to prove it so.

> A farmer brought to the county fair a pumpkin shaped exactly like a one gallon pickle jar. When he was asked how he grew such a perfectly formed pumpkin, he said that when the pumpkin started to grow, he put it into a pickle jar. The pumpkin grew into the shape of the container and then he just broke the jar.

Your mind has the same capacity to be molded into the shape of what you think about. You shape your mind and then your thoughts shape you.

Consider the fact that today is all you really have. You don't own yesterday, nor can you bank on tomorrow. The now is all you can control, and by shaping your now you can change or influence your tomorrows.

LIVING THE PLAN

Think through some of the days in your life that are especially meaningful to you. What made those moments so special?

Do you agree that having another special or "high water mark" day will not diminish from those days you have already experienced? Why or why not?

Do you tend to react or respond to events that come into your life?

Have you ever experienced the truth that you can change your life when you change your thinking? If so, when was that? If not, are you willing to take the challenge to discover what will happen if you change your thinking?

What lessons do you take away from the parable of the pickle jar?

2.

ONE DAY AT A TIME

Therefore do not worry about tomorrow,
for tomorrow will worry about itself.
Each day has enough trouble of its own.
Matthew 6:34

Jesus told His disciples in Matthew 6:34, not to be anxious and worry about the future. He was telling them (and you) to focus on one day at a time, the present day. You are not to dwell on the past or be anxious about the future. Jesus is clearly saying to live fully, one day at a time, live completely in the present.

Living fully, today, one day at a time is the best way to successfully navigate your life. Many times, there is an event, which on the surface does not look like there will be a good outcome, but in reality, something good does come of it.

> *In 1980, the founder of Mothers Against Drunk Driving; Candy Lightner, took the tragic event of her 13 year old daughter's death at the hands of a repeat drunk driving offender and made something positive*

come out of it. Since the time she started M.A.D.D., the organization has saved countless lives that might have otherwise been lost. Candy did not waste her energy on worrying about what might have been or excessively grieving the past. She made something good come from a very difficult and tragic experience.

Today is the Day. It is the only one you have. You have no guarantee that there will be a tomorrow for you. Life gives you no guarantees. You probably don't regularly dwell on the transitory nature of life, that you are going to die, but it is the reality you face each day.

You could make a commitment to live today as if it were the only day you had. Determining that today will be the best day ever frees you to live completely in the moment. You have not have time to worry about yesterday or fret about tomorrow. You can live this day as if it were your last. You can live it with no regrets and no worrying about tomorrow. You can live with the idea that what you need to do you will do today and not wait for another day. Today is the day; do it today.

When you think about it, as a human being living today, you are locked in a Time-Space-Matter vortex. This vortex of earth is much like an aquarium. In this illustration, you are like fish in the aquarium and you have choices. You could be a wise fish, choosing to swim and frolic, living fully and abundantly in the now that is the aquarium. Or, you could be a foolish fish, looking outside the aquarium where you cannot swim, wishing you could jump into the future, or relive the past.

These foolish fish are missing out on today's unique opportunities:

Foolish Fish

Past Wishers	Future Wishers
You can look through the glass, on one side of the aquarium, and see the past.	You look out through the foggy glass at what may be.
You choose to focus on the side where you watch the past go by.	You wonder what may come to pass and what you might do in the future.
You dwell on what might have been and/or long for the familiarity of the past.	You are waiting for some ideal time.

Yes, you can and should look back from time to time on your history and how far you have come, and you should look to the future and plan your goals (end game). But, you must live in the now. You must live in the moment; it is the only aquarium that you have and if you try to live outside the aquarium, you are, well, like a fish out of water.

Failures in the Past

If you think about it, living one day at a time is the only way you can live. You just physically can't live in any other way. Living in the present is also the only *sane* way to live. Obsessing over past hurts or opportunities missed is not a mentally healthy practice. If you dwell on the unresolved issues of your past you are destined to spend today on the therapist's couch and not living fully and freely as a healthy person. Dwelling on yesterday is not a productive or healthy way to live and it is not a very good use of the time that you do have.

You are the expert on you. As you consider your life, learn to put the earlier hurts and events of the past aside. They are, after all, in the past. They only have power in your now, if you allow them to possess you. Don't empower the past to do damage to the present.

Problems in the Future

In the same way, don't fret about tomorrow, worrying about what might happen. Don't enable your fears and anxiety. Living in the future, in the hopes that something will change for the best, is dysfunctional. You mortgage your present for a future that will probably never arrive. Use that energy for the now, living freely and abundantly in the now, making today the best day of your life.

When you live one day at a time, you are freed from the concern of having to save or conserve energy for the future. You can put the pedal to the metal and go for it with all the gusto you have. You are not saving some energy in reserve for a future that may never arrive, you are using all your energy, every day, to make this one day the best day of your life.

> **Sometimes it is good to confide in a friend or counselor who will listen and reflect back to you what your heart is telling your mind.**

Potential of the Present

Living one day at a time does not mean you fail to plan. You still need to plan and set goals, but to understand **the achievement of goals can only come through living out each day at a time**. Your goals are progressively realized in the accomplishment of each day. The accumulation of these successful days will propel your dreams and visions into reality. Goals are future oriented, you can't touch them today, but you can build steps today toward reaching your goals.

You should consider each day a success if in some way you have moved closer to your preferred future. You will not achieve your future goals every day, but every day you must live in such a way that you move closer to those goals. There is a destination (goal) and there is a journey (steps toward a goal). Both of these are part of the process for creating a successful life.

So, how can you live fully and abundantly in the present, and keep from dwelling in the past or obsessing about the future?

- *Consider* why some events are torpedoing your best day ever. Then you will be able to deal with those events in a positive and proactive way.
- *Commit* to live fully in the present. When you make this commitment it becomes very clear when you waste time in the past or future. You can stop yourself when you see it happening and evaluate what events are trying to keep you from living in the now.

It will be different for each person, but like Shakespeare said, "Know thyself. Be true to thyself." In other words, speak the truth to yourself.

If you really thought about it, you would never waste time thinking about the past or worrying about the future. Living one day at a time—the present day—is the only way you can live. Yesterday is past, tomorrow never comes. All you have is the present moment. Living one day at a time, the current day, is the only way you can influence the future or build a history and legacy. Today is that day. The Bible says in Hebrews 3:13 to encourage one another while it is still called, "Today." In other words, you are not to put off doing good until some future time, but to do good today.

LIVING THE PLAN

Do you tend to dwell in the past, present, or future?

Think on the Past	Live in the Present	Worry about the Future
What events or memories trigger past regrets?	What would you want your last day to look like?	What concerns fuel your anxiety about tomorrow?
If you could give up those memories, would you do it?	What steps can you take today to live more fully in the present?	If you could give up those concerns, would you do it?
What is in the past you wish was still present?		What are you currently experiencing that you would like to be free from in the future?
What will it take for you to make today the best day of your life?		

Since you alone carry these memories and concerns, you are the one responsible to deal with them. No one is making you feel the way you do, that is your choice.

3.

TIME IS RELATIVE

"There is a season for everything under heaven, a time…"
Ecclesiastes 3:1

What is time? Simply put, time is the function of your current reality that keeps everything from happening all at once. Time separates and measures the events in your lives. Time is relative in that it moves in relationship to your measure of reality. You say things like, "Where has the time gone?" or, "The time goes so quickly." Time, given your current reality, is truly a space-time continuum.

Bodies move in a confined, finite space and time keeps everything from happening at once. In the brief moment a "second" appears and then is gone, another one takes its place. When the span of a second or a minute or hour is over, it is gone forever. Confucius said that you can never step in the same stream twice. This is true in so far as the water moves, the stream changes. So also, with the passing of time you change. You can never live the same minute over again. You have one life to live, moment by moment.

Life is for living in the moment, not being overly concerned with time or age, but living each day as if it were your last, fully and freely, no regrets, living today as the best day of your life. Someone wrote, "Life is not measured by the number of breaths you take, but by the moments that take your breath away."

Many people who are lying on their deathbeds are willing to pay anything for just a little more time. Often when it is too late, you realize that you have squandered your life. You have wasted your time on trivial pursuits and majoring on the minors. You probably do this: you go along and before you know it, you have no idea of where the time has gone.

Ask a person what they would do with more time and most will tell you, "I donno." The average person in America watches entirely too much TV and spends an inordinate amount of time playing on the internet or video games. Observing this behavior, Neil Postman said, Americans are "amusing ourselves to death."

Wise with What You Have

You do not need more time. You need to be wise about the time that you have. You have all the time you need. Every person gets the same 24 hours in a day from the president to the janitor. (Trust me on this, I have been the leader of organizations and also worked my way through high school and college as a janitor. I never received more or less than 24 hours in any day my entire life, no matter what I was doing or what title I held.) You are given the same allotment of time as anyone else, but you may not invest your time in the same way. Some people actually call it, "spending time," as if it were a commodity that could be bought, sold or saved up.

Time cannot be bought or sold, at any price. I was in a bookstore recently with my wife. She asked if I needed anything in the store. I looked around at all the books and I was a bit overwhelmed. "You know," I said, "If they could figure out a way to sell some time so I had the opportunity to read more books, I would go for that!" (Obviously that will never happen.) My wife gave me that look that says, "You have all the time you need, you just need to use your time more wisely."

She is right of course: you just need to use the time you have more wisely. Time cannot be saved or invested, however, wasting time, well, that is clearly a viable option. Most of us have squandered or wasted some precious moments of our lives. Have you ever left a movie theatre and felt that you should be reimbursed for the several hours that you just wasted on a lousy film?

What is Waste?

Wasting time is relative. Charles F. Adams was the grandson of John Adams and son of John Quincy Adams. He served as a Massachusetts state senator, a US Congressman and ambassador to Great Britain under Abraham Lincoln. He was also very conscientious about keeping a daily journal and encouraged his seven children to do the same.

Henry Brooks, the fourth of Charles children, followed his father's advice and began journaling at a young age. On a particular day when he was eight, he made this entry in his journal:

> *"Went fishing with my father today, the most glorious day of my life."*

The day was so magnificent, in fact, that Henry continued to talk and write about that particular day for the next thirty years. One day he decided to compare his journal entry with that of his father. Of that same day, Charles had written:

"Went fishing with my son, a day wasted."

One of the many blessings in life is that you get to determine how you use your time and how you evaluate the time "spent." Henry and Charles certainly had a different paradigm and process for determining the value of a day spent fishing together!

Managing Margins

Wasting time is different than inserting or building margins into your lives. You need to consider "down time" or margins in and around your lives. You can't just bounce from one event or appointment to another. You need to pencil in space between events, a time to recharge or a time to prepare for the next event.

It is very disconcerting, especially when you are talking with a counselor or lawyer, to see someone constantly checking their watch because they are expecting another paying customer. People like this are slaves to time and they have not learned that time is relative and you have the power to harness time to your advantage. A little time management can be a great asset and it includes building margins into your schedules.

LIVING THE PLAN

Have you ever heard or used the expression, "It's about TIME"? What does that mean to you?

Where have you found yourself "wasting" time?

What would you do with "more time"?

> *A good time management technique is to prioritize your to-do list and do the most important one first. Try it! As much as possible finish one project before going on to the next one. If you have to start back up on a cold project you expend additional time getting up to speed or to the place where you left off.*

Have you ever felt concern for your advancing years? What do you feel is the root of the fear of getting older?

If you did not know how old you were, how old do you think you would feel?

There is a time for everything the writer of Ecclesiastes tells us. Are you scheduling time for rest, recreation, exercise, eating healthy and avoiding stress and burnout? Are you burning the candle at both ends? How can you find more balance in your schedule?

What do you need to schedule time for today? This week? This month?

4.

LESSONS FROM THE GRAVEYARD

*"You do not know what your life will be like tomorrow.
You are just a vapor that appears for a little while and then
vanishes away."*
James 4:14

A human life begins, continues for a space of time, and then ends. To be alive means you have been born and that one day you will die. My son says, "**You are immortal until you die.**" Dying is currently an outcome of living.

You probably do not dwell daily on the fact that you will die. You might not even think about the subject until you drive by a cemetery or hear of someone dying. Death then interrupts your thinking. Perhaps, it is at this time that the reality of death and your own mortality reminds you that you are human and that life as you know it will end.

These times when death interrupts your thinking can be positive markers to help you remember that you truly only have one day to live. Recognizing the reality of death can sharpen your resolve to "do it today," and to make today the best day of your life.

I have watched children being readied for bed. They fight and resist going to bed and I have wondered if they see the cessation of their day as a kind of death. They don't know what the night will bring or what is on the other side. However, I have seen children who also go to be and do not resist, they are tired and lay down to a comfortable restful sleep. These kids give us an analogy. You can resist death and the putting down of your toys or you can peacefully embrace the sleep as a reward for your playing so hard.

In order to face death unafraid, and to take the sting and pain out of death, you really do need to begin with the end in mind. What do you want on your tombstone? How do you want to be remembered? A big part of preparing for death is determining how you are going to live each day.

Fear of the Unknown

Most people will choose a difficult known situation rather than face the fear of an unknown situation. The familiar, the known, is preferable to the unfamiliar and unknown. This makes change making in your life very difficult. You often need a change from where you are, but you are reticent to do anything proactive, torpedoing yourself, again, so that you will not have to face the fear of the unknown.

Death is a huge unknown. There is not a lot of data and research available for you to have built up a knowledge base. Precious few people have come back from the grave to give eyewitness accounts. Making peace with death is an important function of healthy living.

You will not thrive if you are scared that at any moment you could die. Of course the reality and truth is that you are only a heartbeat away from dying at any moment. You do not have any security, or any reassurance, that you will live out even one day. It is unhealthy and morbid to dwell on death. But it is very freeing and empowering to have the question of death settled in your heart once and for all. That is why it is so important that you take the sting out of death, that you personally deal with the issue of your own mortality, and literally put death to rest.

Putting Fears to Rest

Spirituality, and sometimes religion, are part of the answer to death. Spirituality is a part of the human condition and it is often denied by people who feel they don't need anything to do with religion. Ironically, a person who is spiritually alive, and in touch with their own spirituality, is a typically well-rounded and an often solid person.

Organized religion has helped some people develop their sensitivity toward their own spirituality. You read of the desert fathers and the journals and writings of holy men and women and you see a depth of life that would not be there if the spiritual component was not engaged.

Religion and spirituality are not necessarily the same thing and there is some need to clarify these distinctions. However, suffice it to say that religious people are generally more spiritually astute and they will most likely be the ones who have settled the question of death, mortality and the afterlife.

LIVING THE PLAN

How do you feel when you hear James 4:14; *"You do not know what your life will be like tomorrow. You are just a vapor that appears for a little while and then vanishes away"* ?

How do you want to be remembered?

Write an epitaph for your tombstone or write out your obituary. Include what you wish to be remembered for, even if it is not your current reality.

How as the fear of the unknown kept you from accomplishing your desires?

5.

DO IT TODAY

"But encourage one another daily, as long as it is called today."
Hebrews 3:13a

Many years ago I was on the staff of the downtown Church of the Open Door in Los Angeles. Because it was a very old and established church, many leaders and workers were afraid of doing something for fear they were going to go against tradition. I had so many people coming to me asking for permission to do various things, that were clearly within their job descriptions, that I finally put a plaque on my desk that read, "Just do it!" (What I failed to do, however, was copyright the phrase!) When people came into my office to ask permission to do their job, I would point to the sign, affirm my support and let them know that the past was not going to dictate the future.

Recently, I saw a tee shirt that proclaimed, "I'm doing it!" The phrase is timeworn now and it means different things to different people, but the root idea is still very powerful and empowering. **Just do the thing you are thinking about doing. Just do the thing that you are avoiding or putting off doing.**

What is it you have been putting off? What do you know you need to do or get done? If you think about it, you are more stressed by the things you *don't* do than by the things *you do*. You avoid the difficult phone call or confrontation, you put off the tasks that you dislike or that you find unfulfilling or not enjoyable. These tasks that you try to suppress or avoid actually burn up more energy than if you had gone ahead and simply gotten the job done in the first place.

When you live with the attitude of, "do it today" your lives take on a simple beauty and you find that you are not stressing out as much as you used to. Not only are you not stressing, but others can count on you. Let's look at Boaz. (His story is found in the book of Ruth.) He was an honorable man, a good man and a good businessman. He made a covenant with his relatives to take Ruth as his wife. Naomi told her daughter- in-law that Boaz was the type of man who would not rest that day until he had settled any outstanding matters. Boaz was a man with a positive reputation. He did marry Ruth and together they became ancestors in the family line of Jesus of Nazareth.

When you (and I) determine not to procrastinate, put off undesirable tasks or wait for tomorrow to get a job done, you are carrying the weight of that uncompleted task for yet another day. In order for this to be the very best day of your life, you need to get into the habit of not putting off for tomorrow what you could do today.

> *Joshua's car needed fixed but he just didn't get "around to it." His wife was gently encouraging him to get it done, although he called it "nagging." Finally, he did take the car in to have the repairs done and it made a world of difference. Not only*

was his wife no longer pleading with him to get the work done, but the car was performing better as well. He told me that what he did not expect was the freedom that came from getting the job completed. It felt as though an anchor chain that was wrapped around his neck was gone. He was no longer carrying the burden of unfinished business.

When you decide to live as if this were the last day you had, to accomplish today what you have been putting off, you ironically find a new energy and strength to get the tasks done.

Alexander Pope wrote that "fools rush in where angels fear to tread." The world is full of successful "fools," people that did not know something was not possible so they went ahead and did the thing anyway. These are the record breakers and the over-achievers. The world may call them fools, but it is rather harsh to call someone a fool when they simply didn't know that everyone else was paralyzed.

"Do it today," could be your new mantra. Say it over and over and encourage yourself to make the effort to do the thing today. My father used to tell me, **"If you don't have time to do it right, when are you going to have the time to do it over?"** My dad was not as concerned with doing the right thing as he was with doing the thing right. (Yes, he was a perfectionist and he graciously and liberally shared this DNA with me.)

Perfectionist Paralysis

Perfectionists won't even start something if they think the finished product will not be perfect at the end. The sin of perfectionism (and I am relativity certain it is one of the seven deadly sins) derails people from even starting good projects and finishing great plans.

Later in life, I read this quote from G. K. Chesterton, who is one of my all time favorite authors. He said, "Anything worth doing is worth doing poorly." In all my life I had never heard it put that way. I was always taught to do the best I possibly could in whatever I started. But there is a simple truth in what Chesterton observed. Sometimes you can't do your best but that should not stop you from trying.

Chesterton message to us is like a parent teaching their children good habits. Is a child brushing their teeth a good thing? Of course. Then even if a child brushed poorly, it is better that they brush than if they had not brushed at all. Well, when you put it like that, it does makes sense. So anything worth doing is worth doing poorly if the option is never doing the thing at all.

The idea of putting off for tomorrow what you should do today puts your life on hold. You are again loosing out on all that life has for you today. For whatever reason you tell yourself you are procrastinating.

When it comes to making today the best day of your lives, do you stop short and say, "Maybe tomorrow"? But tomorrow never comes. Do it today.

LIVING THE PLAN

Just for today, do what you need to do.

What tasks have you been putting off? Why?

Since this is going to be the best day of your life, do those things you keep putting off. Notice how freeing it is to have it done. What a relief to have just done it.

One good time management technique is to "Do it now." When you procrastinate, you are setting yourself up for failure on several levels. Do you remember what my dad used to say? What things are you putting off for a later time? Why?

Letter to write, card to send. Don't miss an opportunity to say a kind word or build someone up. (When I had my piano tuned, I was SO impressed: It turned out like new! I shared my experience on Facebook and the piano tuner told me he got some referrals from my posting.) Everyone wins when you just do it today.

Do you agree that anything worth doing is worth doing poorly? When has the fear of failure kept you from trying?

Is a failure the person who tries and does not make it, or the person who never tries for fear they will fail?

What would you accomplish if you knew you would not fail?

6.

YOU ARE UNIQUE

"For You created my inmost being; You knit me together in my mother's womb. I praise You because I am fearfully and wonderfully made; Your works are wonderful, I know that full well. My frame was not hidden from You when I was made in the secret place, when I was woven together in the depths of the earth. "
Psalm 139:13-15

In all the world you are the only one of you.

> Billions of people have lived and are living and you are unique in all the world and all the universe!
>
> No one has your fingerprints; no one is exactly like you.
>
> You are unique, one of a kind, and therefore very special.
>
> You are an individual. There is only one. No other person can think your thoughts, write the way you write, draw like you draw, or do a hundred other things like you do.
>
> You are unique; you are somebody very special.

A creative teacher had her students ink one of their thumbs and put their thumbprint in the middle of a piece of paper. The children were to write their names on the paper and use some descriptive words to let others know something about their life. Then each student was to incorporate the thumbprint into a self portrait. Lastly, she put all her student's artwork on the bulletin board which was titled; "I'm Thumb body." No two pieces of art were alike, they were as different and diverse as her class and she clearly made the point that every student was different; every person was somebody unique and very special.

Obviously, this special teacher was unique. It is a strange paradox that much of education is concerned about conformity instead of valuing individuality. While society seems to value the maverick, it is conformity that is rewarded in school. You see this paradox in young people who want so badly to be seen as a unique individual and they will go to any length to look and act like their peers. And adults are as guilty as the younger generation when it comes to conformity. Mimicking others to prove ones' individuality never made much sense to me. Perhaps it was the way I was raised, but I have always distrusted herd mentality and sought to be my own person and think my own thoughts.

There is an interesting news story that can be found on the Internet about a town in Turkey where, in 2005, a herd of sheep were grazing on a hill. The shepherds had gone to town to eat lunch and from their vantage point they watched in shock, as one sheep jumped over the cliff and then 1,500 other sheep followed![3]

We call this type of behavior "Lemming mentality. " If one does it, then everyone has to do it. Have you ever had your son, daughter or young person say, "But all the kids are doing it"? A friend of mine told me that she tried this approach with her mother once when she wanted to go to an un-chaperoned party. She told her mom that all the kids were going to be there and if she didn't go she would just die. Her mother replied, "Well you are not going and I am not everyone's mother."

One day, I was driving my son and some of his friends to pizza for his birthday. I was listening to their conversation as I drove and I heard the boys all agreeing on something. Then, kindly and sincerely, my son disagreed with all of his peers. I was admittedly proud of him that day because he did not go along with the gang simply because they were his friends. I knew then and there that the values my wife and I tried to instill in our children were being rooted in their lives.

Conformity is encouraged in almost every society. The person who sticks out or is a true individual is discouraged and suspect. In the opening scene to Disney's animated movie, "Beauty and the Beast," Belle is walking through the town as the entire village focuses on how much she is different. This difference is considered culturally wrong simply because she is different. Sadly, this movie mirrors what happens in real life.

Whether it is water conforming to the shape of the object, which holds it, or a pumpkin growing in a pickle jar, people are

---

3 The rest of the story: While this event was devastating to the economy of the villagers of Gevas, Turkey, who all owned part of the herd, the remarkable thing was that almost a thousand sheep, two thirds, survived the jump because they were cushioned by the third of the flock that leaped first and died!

also pressed into conformity with societies norms. Society and the world are trying to squeeze you into its mold (or mould-either is correct.) People are being socialized in school, business and elsewhere to conform. People who are non-creative, predictable and normal citizens are valued as they have been pressed into the cookie cutter of conformity. Again, it is utterly amazing to think that the norm is conformity, sameness and uniformity when the reality, the underlying true truth, is that every person is an individual. Every person is unique and completely different in every way from everyone else.

When you think about the fact that you are unique, but forces around you are trying to squeeze you into conformity, you realize that expressing your individuality is truly a freeing experience. You are different from every one of the billions of inhabitants living today or who have lived in the past. You need to celebrate your uniqueness. You are unique in the entire world throughout all time. There will never be another person just like you and the world is waiting for your unique and special contribution. Today is that day.

Societal Deprecation

In our current, American way of life, life is not sacred; it is common. People are not valued in our culture; they are devalued. Movies and violent videogames feed a self-centered society. Sex and human trafficking, abortion on demand, rape and murder all indicate a culture that devalues human life. The cheapening of human life destroys the human spirit and is dehumanizing and debilitating.

You need to learn how to resist the culture that suggests you are a common person. In order to counter this demoralizing force, one in which you may not even be aware, you can to remember that you are unique in all the world. I saw a bumper sticker that read, "Be yourself, everyone else is taken." There is so much truth in that little phrase.

Remember that you are the only expert on you. You have choices and you have the right, responsibility and privilege to make your life anything you wish it to be. You can decide how you live your life, and what you do and what you think. You have the ability to weigh the consequences and to make decisions. You can't always control what happens to you, but you can control your response and how you frame those experiences of life. Choose wisely and choose to make today the very best day of your life.

LIVING THE PLAN

Do you agree that you are totally unique? Do you really, truly believe it?

How have you been trapped into conformity to someone else's standards?

When have you been tempted to follow the herd?

When have you wanted to be different and demonstrate your individuality?

How would embracing your individuality free you to make today the best day of your life?

7.

TRUTH AND FREEDOM

"You will know the truth and the truth will set you free."
John 8:32

Standing before a group of graduate students, I thought how best to facilitate their discussions. I was their professor, in charge of teaching leadership and ethics. But, I confess I was at a loss as to how to conduct our study of absolute truth when I had students telling me that their truth may be different from my truth. They were confusing truth with reality.

In this culture, some people don't really understand positional truth or the difference between what is true and what is not true. I made an effort to explain that truth is always truth. At the same time, your perception, your reality, can change over time or differ from someone else's perception. It is true that my reality is different than anyone else's reality, but truth is always true. That is part of the definition of truth:

> *Conformity or in agreement with fact, something proven as an actuality. An established principle, fixed*

law, exact accordance with that which is.

Reality on the other hand is less objective, more subjective and more a matter of personal experience.

An idea, notion, or conception. Discernable by the mind.

So, there is a big difference between truth and reality, and what role they can play in your life. True truth sets you free, but your perceptions, your reality, your beliefs can often make you captive, prisoners in your own mind.

In living today as the best day of your life, you should want to live free, unencumbered by falsehood, lies or untruths. Over the years, I've developed the idea of "freedom factors." These freedom factors are so important that the next four chapters will each deal with one of them.

The freedom factors are:

The Freedom of Forgiveness
The Freedom of Finances
The Freedom from Filth (polluting the mind)
The Freedom from Furnishings (possessions)

Freedom of Forgiveness. *Accept forgiveness and forgive others.*

If you have truly experienced forgiveness by God, then it should be much easier to find it in your hearts to forgive someone else. Conversely, if you have never experienced His forgiveness it is much harder to extend forgiveness to others. In a parable, Jesus taught us the importance of forgiving others, especially when you've been forgiven. Jesus told of a servant who owed His master a huge sum, almost a million dollars. He begged forgiveness and his master forgave the debt. Then, the servant went out and found a man that owed him something like a hundred dollars and he had the man arrested until he could pay the debt. Word of this got around to the master and you can imagine how ticked he was at this unforgiving servant.

God has forgiven you and me. He paid a debt He did not owe because you owed a debt you could not pay. When you understand the significance of God's forgiveness, how can you hold unforgiveness in your heart? Someone said, "Unforgiveness is the poison you give yourself." Having unforgiveness in your heart only pollutes you; it does nothing to the person who offended you. Therefore, I like what one person wrote: **"Forgiveness is a gift you give yourself."**

Many books and articles about forgiveness have been written and some with conflicting information. This book gives some guidance on the issue of learning to forgive and move on, but I also wrote another book called: "A Time to Forgive." If this is an issue that is holding you back from experiencing the best day of your life, I would encourage you to get the book and go though the exercises.

Freedom of Finances

It is odd really, that you live in one of the richest countries on the globe and more and more people complain that they don't have enough money, or possessions. Credit card debt is just out of control in our country. Fewer and fewer people are debt free. My wife and I are facilitators for Dave Ramsey's Financial Peace University and Legacy Journey. Of course, we highly recommend the Ramsey material and plan. (I can't unpack the whole plan for you today, but this book can get you started, and you can certainly go online and find a Financial Peace University meeting near your home.) We have worked through the plan ourselves and not only have we experienced the freedom of being debt free, but we also led our church to finally pay off their mortgage and becoming debt free.

When you are fretting about money every day it is hard to have your best day ever. That is why you can move toward your goal of being debt free and still experience the best day of your life today. As long as you are daily working toward achieving your goals, success will one day come, as it must.

There are two things you can do to become debt free:

- *Spend wisely.* Live within your means. Prioritize, budget, and wait patiently. You can have the best day of your life by waiting patiently instead of going out and purchasing what you want when you want it.
- *Increase income.* You can be creative on this one. You can take on a second job until you are out of debt. Or, you can make yourself more valuable to your own company by taking on more responsibility, or taking classes and increasing your skills. Or, you can move to a new, better paying job. You could even turn your hobby into a business. You have options.

Have your money work for you, instead of you working for money.

Freedom from Filth

Your mind needs to be protected as much as your body does. You probably would never think of stepping on the tracks of an oncoming train. You love yourself too much to do that. But what about the train wrecks in your mind: stepping in front of the TV or computer screen, and allowing all sorts of filth and mental pollution to enter your lives?

Paul writes in the book of Romans that you need to stop becoming conformed to this world, which means not letting your mind be shaped and pressed into the world's mold. (Incidentally there are two ways to spell mold here, and they are both correct when it comes to the world's mold, or mould.) Paul further encourages you to be transformed, by the renewing of your mind. Your mind needs to be transformed, like a caterpillar's metamorphous into a butterfly. You need to experience the process of transformation and renewal in your minds.

You are allowing your mind to be shaped by this world's thinking, rather than God's word, when you go to bed listening to the news, or you always have the TV on, or you have to go to the latest movies or rent the latest videos, without any thought to screening the media first. You are shaping your mind's reality but not being shaped and set free by the truth. You can't pollute your minds by the influences of the world and expect to have your best day ever.

> I have a very discerning daughter, and she constantly filters what she reads, sees and hears through a Biblical filter. She doesn't understand how other people don't see what she sees, or how they take what they're told as fact. Being wise with our time includes being wise in how we view things.

Set your mind free by filling it with truth. You need to be free from the weights and burdens of mental distress. If you are feeling bondage in this area, I would urge you to get professional help from either your pastor or a Christian counselor. While there is no substitute for having a professional guide, there are many books on getting free from the bondage of pornography, metaphysical teachings, cults and all sorts of counterfeits and landmines the enemy of your soul places in your path each day.

Freedom from Furnishings

Free yourself from the problem of clutter: Possessions. They are called possessions because after you have paid a lot of money for them they posses you. You also call them collectables because they collect dust, rust and decay.

Hoarding is a terrible problem in your society and it is keeping many people from living healthy, fulfilling and free lives. Have you seen the show, "Hoarders"? At some point in this pathology you become your stuff. And this is where Jesus' words are so timely; the Living Bible puts it this way: "Life is not measured by how much you own." You can throw things out without feeling that you are throwing out a part of your life.

Clutter works itself into your life and begins to cost us in emotional energy, time, effort and expenses. Look at all the storage facilities people rent per square foot, monthly. Some people would be better off renting an apartment and storing all their stuff there instead of a heated storage facility. And have you seen some of the stuff people save and store?

I had some friends who moved out of their home and into a fifth wheel so they could tour the country. After their yard sale, I helped them store all the things that they just could not part with. Fifteen years later, we emptied the storage locker to find old and/or ruined items where their belongings used to be. With the money they spent storing the items, they could have bought new things. Of the more irreplaceable collectables, most were damaged, eaten by rodents and infested with bugs.

It was all rotting, rusting and decaying. Not a pretty sight.

Jesus warned us not to store up treasures on earth in Matthew 6:19-21. It is really a passage about guarding your heart, though. Notice, He said, where you treasure is, there your heart will be also. **You need to treasure your relationships, not your stuff**. Do not worry about your junk or be burdened by clutter. Become clutter free, laying up treasure in heaven. After all you can't take your stuff with you when you die (but, apparently, your good works can be sent on ahead in the form of treasures in heaven, Revelation 22:12).

Live Free in Truth

You have the tremendous opportunity to live free today. Free from an unforgiving heart, free from the love of money and the love of possessions. You are free from being captive to filth and mind pollution. You can live free today and live today as the best day of your life. Treasure each day, living each day as the best day ever.

LIVING THE PLAN

Do you recognize the difference between truth and reality?

Can you tell the difference between truth and reality in your life?

Which "Freedom Factor" do you have the most trouble? Why do you think you struggle in that area?

Do you know of others who are struggling in each of the four areas? Can you put a person's name beside each of the four "Freedom Factors?" *It may be helpful to think of people who struggle in these areas as you work through the information in the next four chapters.*

Each of the four factors is a heart issue. Over and over you are told to guard your heart. How could you guard your heart in response to each of four factors?

8.

FREEDOM OF FORGIVENESS

Forgive us our debts as we have forgiven our debtors.
Matthew 6:12

Unresolved forgiveness issues can keep you from experiencing the best day of your life. In order to really live each day to it's fullest potential, you and I can't be carrying around the burden and chains of unforgiveness.

Situations, circumstances, your perceptions, your feelings: You process all of these through your own unique filter. Many different people in diverse situations have worked with me to go through the healing process of forgiveness. In most cases, those who really wanted to be set free found the freedom that comes from true forgiveness. To initiate change, in the area of forgiveness, there are certain principles that can be followed. (If you want to explore this topic in more depth, I have a thorough examination of the subject in my book, *"A Time to Forgive."*) Examine your life through the filter of true forgiveness.

Let's be clear what forgiveness is NOT:

- Ignoring, overlooking or disregarding a wrong done.
- It is not excusing or justifying a person's behavior.
- It is not tolerating evil or closing your eyes to wrongs.
- It is not pretending the issue never happened
- It is not just being nice toward the offending person.

There are two other things that are definitely NOT true forgiveness.

- *Forgiving and forgetting.* It is impossible to forget what happened, especially if it was traumatic. You need to forgive, and remember that you have chosen to forgive.
- *Time heals all wounds.* Often, time is your enemy. Sometimes, not dealing with a wrong for a long time even makes it worse!

With the idea of what forgiveness is not, look at what forgiveness is. How would you define or describe it? Probably the best definition I have heard is; "**Forgiveness is an intentional act that removes from the offending person all blame and guilt and reckons them NOT GUILTY and no longer accountable for the offence.**" What do you feel when you hear that description of forgiveness? Does it sound possible, workable or even thinkable?

That is the awesome beauty of true forgiveness. It is genuinely viewing the offending person as no longer culpable or guilty of the offence. You don't ever again view them as having committed the offence. That means you don't go around bad mouthing or slandering someone who has offended you. You will choose to forgive and remember that you have forgiven. You will probably choose not to get into the same situation with this person again, but you have taken out the sting from your life of getting even with the other person.

You don't have to wait for an apology from that person to forgive someone! You can choose to forgive even before someone says they are sorry or admits their guilt. You must make the first move, because forgiveness is not something you do for the other person necessarily, it is really something that you do for yourself.

Other people are sometimes oblivious to the wrongs they have done, or are in denial about the things they have done. Have you ever noticed someone who suddenly begins to treat you with a lack of respect? They begin to hold a grudge or have something against you, but even when you confront them, they deny that anything is wrong.

Once, when I was working in an office, a female employee began to be cold and aloof with me. I finally learned from someone else that this woman thought I had eaten her lunch from out of the break room refrigerator. (Apparently another employee took it upon himself or herself to throw her lunch away because it had been in the fridge several days and was getting moldy.) I will never forget how this woman handled her perceived grievance against me. She did not proactively deal with the problem, but she carried around her hurt and offence, dwelling on the situation but never dealing with it. She did not confront me, she just told everyone else. She was a captive in the prison of her own thoughts.

This woman thought she was punishing me by treating me with her poor attitude. But, she wasn't hurting me, she was hurting herself! Carrying around an unforgiving spirit does nothing to or for the offender; it only binds the person carrying the offence.

If you truly live each day as the best day of your life, you cannot waste time and energy on a lack of forgiveness. You cannot expend the mental energy to remember everything anyone has done to you. You must live in the complete and total freedom of forgiveness. Does it cost? Sure it does but it is worth it. I have seen, and documented elsewhere, situations that seemed impossible to forgive. These include the homicide of a mother's son, the embezzlement of an entire company's savings, and physical abuse. The offenders in the examples still had to face the consequences and legal implications of their crimes, but the victims chose not to continue to be victimized. The innocent parties remained innocent and did not carry the vendetta of judge, jury and executioner. They chose to forgive and remember that they had forgiven.

A former student of mine now has a ministry called, "Live to Forgive." (I highly recommend his book and video.) When he was young, his baseball bat was used by his step father to bludgeon his mother to death. His step father went to prison for a long time. All that time, this young boy thought of nothing else but growing up strong and tough, and one day killing the man who murdered his mother. I don't want to give a spoiler here, but suffice it to say there was one murder in the family, not two, and forgiveness made the difference. In fact, his forgiveness is continuing to make an incredible difference, even today.

You probably do not have to deal with the cold-blooded murder of your mother, yet you may still be unforgiving when someone wrongs you in a trifle way. If you are carrying around a spirit of unforgiveness I would urge you to get some professional help to work through the principles of forgiveness.

Forgiveness is freeing. If you have ever experienced first hand being forgiven or forgiving someone else, you know how incredibly freeing this experience truly is.   Today, agree with yourself that you will seek to forgive anyone who has offended you. You do not need to seek reconciliation or to insist on them asking for forgiveness. Forgiveness is an intentional act that *you choose* regardless of the attitudes and actions of the offending person.

> *"Forgiveness sets the captive free,*
> *only to find the prisoner was me."*
> ~Dr. Mark von Ehrenkrook

LIVING THE PLAN

Make a list of everyone who has offended you that comes to mind. Go down the list and cross everyone off. You do not need to tell them they are forgiven, you do not need to necessarily confront or seek restitution or reconciliation. This is something you do privately, for yourself, to begin your own healing. Let go of the desire to make that person feel bad.

When a person on the list comes to mind or you meet them, remember that you have crossed their name off the list and you do not carry animosity hatred or any vindictive spirit.

Is there anyone that you need to go to and ask for forgiveness? Make a list of those people of whom you need to be forgiven. Decide on a plan. (It is best not to do it in writing but to ask for forgiveness in person.)

Read a book like "A Time to Forgive" or "Live to Forgive" and seek to incorporate the principles in the book to your own life.

9.

FREEDOM OF FINANCES

"The borrower is slave to the lender. "
Proverbs 22:7

In the movie, *You Can't Take It With You*, one of the underlying themes is the burden of money management. Money is a source of burden for a lot of people. Making money, keeping money, spending money. When you have financial worry in your life, other issues become even more stressful. Financial obligations compound burdens, adding weight to an already intolerable load. Debt crushes the joy out of your life, and you live in a constant state of catching up.

My wife and I have done seminars, workshops, and one-on-one financial counseling with a number of people. However, it was not until we became facilitators with Dave Ramsey's Financial Peace that we really experienced the peace and joy of being debt free.

We took seriously Dave's plan and soon we were completely out of debt, even our house was paid off. Soon after that, I led our church to pay off their mortgage. We have had the pleasure of teaching the Ramsey Financial Peace and Legacy Journey in our city. We highly recommend the principles that Dave teaches and lives.

Now that we have experienced the true freedom of being debt free, we are almost fanatical about sharing the vision with others.

Where You Are

Take a short inventory on where you are, financially free speaking:

YES	NO	ITEM
		I am living financially free today and do not have any financial debt.
		I believe I have full control of my finances and my financial future.
		I am not greedy, miserly, or looking for a get rich quick scheme.
		I have as much money as I currently need.
		I do not self-medicate with money or impulse spending.
		I do not carry a poverty mentality.
		I can handle the debts that I currently owe with collateral.
		I do not go to bed worrying about money concerns.
		I generally understand financial principles.
		I do not indulge in excessive spending.
		I am not covetous of other's lifestyles.
		I have and maintain a personal or household budget.
		I am current with all my bills.
		I limit my investments to my discretionary funds.

		I invest wisely in instruments I can understand.
		I do not have to drive the latest and newest car or truck.
		I am financially content. All I have is all I need and all I need is what I have.
		I freely give to others, the church (tithe), etc. without thought of return or reward.
		I have put my money to work for me.
		I am modeling and instilling these values with those I love.
		I have answered all of these questions honestly.

Financial Problems

There are perhaps three main reasons for financial problems. The first is poor planning. Many couples and individuals do not take the time to seriously budget according to their income. Someone said that a failure to plan is a plan to fail. The laissez-faire way that they approach spending and saving money is a wonderful get poor quick scheme, as Ramsey likes to say.

The second reason is simple ignorance of the foundational financial principles. Why would you put your savings into instruments yielding a half a percent, and be paying off credit cards with the minimum amount each month while incurring over seventeen percent compounded each month?

A third reason for financial problems is the issue of greed and indulgence. In our "me first" society, people expect to have the latest and greatest. Even to suggest to a couple that they get rid of their fifty thousand dollar car with the huge payments and buy something more reasonable, or, suggest they pair down time spent at work to spend more time with their family, they look at me like I am from outer space: "Hey buddy, that doesn't work on this planet. Here you need the status of the expensive car even if you can't afford the gas."

The REAL Problem

In my counseling practice, I have seen many couples that have come in with what we call the "presenting problem," that is, the issue they bring to present to the ever-wise counselor. However, what they present is rarely the real issue. Many times, the presenting problem is described as, "We don't have enough money." But money is rarely the problem; it is a symptom of a deeper issue that usually involves being on the same page mentally.

When a couple is not in agreement with the same values, desires and future outcomes, there will always be conflict to some degree. Money, even the lack of it, is not the real issue. Most couples have "enough" money. Most clients I often see are usually pretty well off, with two incomes, making ten times what their counselor brings home! While I am content with a fraction of their income, I would not want to trade their lifestyle for mine, at any price.

Way to be Debt Free

As I share in counseling, there are two major principles for becoming financially free:

- *Increase your income, if possible.* You need to learn to live within your means. Some ways to increase income is to go back to school and be trained for a new occupation. Or you can see if you have the opportunity to make more money in your current job. How can you be a more valuable employee and therefore be worth more to your employer?

- *Reduce expenses.* Are you using your discretionary income to get out of debt and save for the future, or to increase your standard of living today? A little bit of discipline today will yield incredible dividends in your near future.

Generational Indulgence

Sometimes the indulgence lies with your kids. A few weeks ago, I was with some children in a public setting. One of the little girls pulled out her phone and it was three generations newer than mine. Does a grade school child need that kind of technology? Does she really need the designer jeans and the expensive manicure? Are you indulging your kids because you feel guilty for not spending more time with them? What are you teaching your kids about money and materialism anyway?

It seems you can prolong the financial problem, generationally, by not taking proactive steps in managing your own resources.

Begin at the Beginning

Ever since our first premarital counseling session where we put together a budget, my wife, Susan, and I have been doing budgets, watching our income and expenditures. We have had to be fairly frugal, because we've lived on mainly one income. We have mostly lived on the salary of an associate pastor: Not the most lucrative position, nor a lot of room for pay raises. **Yet, we have learned to live within our means, to plan ahead and save for the things that were important.** To this day, we don't buy the newest cars, or go see the latest movie on opening night. We have always been concerned with being responsible for the money we have.

My three children grew up seeing us living within our budgeted means. When they were in school, we gave each of them a budgeted clothing allowance. It wasn't much, but they were free to supplement their allotment with working after school or picking berries during the summer. We taught them to divide this money they earned into thirds: Church, Savings, Spending. They were free to use the money in their "Spending" piggybank on clothes they would wear. My daughter remembers a time, when she was in second grade, and she couldn't decide whether or not to purchase a warm, purple robe for $8, or to save her $10 for something in the future. My wife helped her walk through the decision-making process, and Amanda had that robe for the next ten years! She learned that investing in something that lasts is beneficial.

In many ways, I am grateful that we didn't have the money to indulge them. From a young age, my children learned to budget, save and shop wisely. As they grew older, they took on more personal financial responsibility. Each one put themselves through college. I thought they would hold a grudge against us if we could not put them through college, but each one has said how much more they valued the experience and the achievement of putting themselves through college and grad school. These were valuable lessons that could not be learned at any price.

Here are some general principles for living financially free:

Start	Finish	ITEM
		Do not purchase on credit any item that depreciates.
		Know the state of your finances every day.
		Make purchases as a couple if you are married.

		Use credit cards like debit cards: never purchase something for which you don't have the cash on hand.
		Make a list when going to the store.
		Seek to simplify your lifestyle.
		Rethink your lifestyle, collections, desires.
		Sell or give away your stuff.
		Avoid infomercials making unrealistic promises. If it is too good to be true, it probably isn't good or it isn't true.
		Limit gift giving
		Set manageable and reachable goals for getting out of debt.
		Make a budget and stick with it.
		Set spending limits for each individual.
		Avoid giving your kids excess, growing an entitlement mentality.

The purpose of making money is not to spend it on your own desires but to leave a legacy to the next generation. When asked how much money a person should seek to make, Pastor Charles Wesley said, "Make as much as you can, save as much as you can and give as much as you possibly can." Billions of dollars will change hands this generation and you have the capacity to make a tremendous impact on the entire world. You will leave a financial heritage, because, you can't take it with you.

LIVING THE PLAN

Take to heart the principles in this chapter. Make and stay on a budget if you do not have one already. Seek to become debt free as soon as possible.

Sign up for Dave Ramsey's Financial Peace workshop and do what he advises in the program. If you are debt free, seriously consider signing up for Ramsey's Legacy Journey workshop.

Follow the suggestions in this chapter, and if you are married seek to get on the same page with your goals and values. Then seek to get on the same page, financially.

Living without the burden of financial pressure is a real blessing. Getting to the point of being debt free is an amazing, and surprisingly short, journey. Each day that you are getting closer to your goal can be the best day of you life!

10.

FREEDOM OF FILTH

"Do not be conformed to the world, but be transformed by the renewing of your minds..."
Romans 12:2a

People live with values and ideas that may have been placed in their minds by others. There is a memory of voices from the past telling a person that they are stupid or worthless and the early imprinting of childhood and youth is often carried over into adulthood. Children and youth usually lack the necessary skills to counter such negative value statements especially when an older, wiser, authority figure says it is so.

In a sense you are conditioned to do this from childhood and you are supposed to learn from those older and wiser. Sadly, this is carried into adulthood, the tapes of the past are played over and over in a person's mind, each time making a deeper and deeper impression like the eroding of the banks of a stream.

School knocks it into your head that you need someone to teach you, you can't just learn on your own. The teacher is right and you are right only as you parrot the learned teacher. You won't even go into what typical education does to children in terms of their creativity, imagination and wonder. So by the time you are educated, you have been beaten down and told to be quiet and regurgitate the correct answers to the tests. Your original thoughts are not valued, not even in your masters or doctoral programs. After being educated, it is truly amazing that you can think at all!

And so, you are conditioned to believe the expert opinion on yourself. Who is really the expert on your life? You are of course. Yet, you allow others to tell you how you should or should not act, what you should wear and how high you should jump. Stop listening to people who pretend to be experts on your lives.

Why don't you trust your own inner voice and accept the fact that you know far more about you than anyone else? Try this exercise: sit down and write out some of your inner dialogue and then evaluate. Replay these words and ask, "Who said so? Who planted that idea? Where did it come from and why am I continuing to believe this about myself?"

Who said it? Is it true? My voice is the most important one for me. Your own inner voice is the most important one for you. You alone are the expert on you. Listen to the assessment of others whom you trust, but do not seek their approval or value. Be in charge of your own self-image.

My high school advisor said I was not smart enough to go into pre med. Even now, decades later, I can still hear her voice, but now, my voice is now also present. When I hear her voice tell me that I am not smart enough, I simply tell her that her assessment was wrong. I don't blame her. I am just sorry for all the other students who took her pronouncement of their lives as the truth. I am capable, and I have an earned doctorate to prove it.

You are a remarkable person and will not be led by the opinions of others, but you will listen to your voice, taking control of your life and living the best day of you life today.

LIVING THE PLAN

What areas of your mind do you think need to be transformed and renewed?

Write down your inner dialogue or self talk that you hear such as, "You can't afford that." "You don't deserve that." "Eat all you want—it's ok."

After you have collected some inner voice phrases, ask yourself who planted those ideas or thoughts. Do they even sound like the voice of parents or teachers when you hear them? How often do you hear positive affirmation?

Consider how negative self talk undermines your happiness and living your best day ever.

Commit to new self-talk and committing positive affirmations to memory. Counter negative self-talk with positive affirmation of your own choosing and determine to reprogram your mind for success.

11.

FREEDOM OF POSESSIONS

"Life does not consist in the abundance of possessions."
Jesus Christ in *Luke 12:15*

One aspect of life that really keeps people from living their best day ever is the problem of clutter. Junk spills over into your closets, garages, crawl spaces, attics, basements and your lives. Eventually many people end up renting very expensive storage areas in which to put their stuff. (Most of these places rent for more money than the junk they hold is worth!) You can call these precious treasures, "possessions" not because you possess them, but because they possess you! You could also call them "collectables" due in part to how much you over-paid for them, but also because they end up "collecting" dust, rust and decay.

You are not Your Stuff

Some people feel they have to stay home and keep their junk safe. When they do venture out, it is to bring in more stuff, and sooner or later they are buried in garbage, powerless to dejunk and declutter. People hoard and clutter up their lives for

57

different reasons, but eventually a line is crossed and people see themselves as their possessions. Somehow in this pathology to give away, sell, or throw out clutter is to destroy a part of themselves. Jesus made it clear that, *"Life does not consist in the abundance of possessions."* The Living Bible puts it this way, *"Life is not measured by how much you own."* You are not your things!

Unfortunately, for too many people most of their prized junk becomes emotional baggage, a weight that gets so heavy that it chokes off their ability to live today, the best day of their lives.

A Time and Place for Everything

I want to get truly sick of having too much stuff. My goal, until I am clutter free, is a bag of junk each day to toss or give away. When I purchase something, I need to get rid of something of at least the same size. Everything I have should have a place to store where I can find it easily. My dad always said, "A place for everything and everything in its place."

Junk does expand to fill the space available, so don't create more space with additional shelving. Seek to get rid of the cabinets or shelves that are taking up your living space. My wife and I have done this with our books and bookshelves and it is tremendously freeing to get back space and to know your books are being enjoyed by others.

You should regularly declutter your life. Think of it as space gaining. This has been a real challenge to me, I usually don't throw out anything, as I never met a piece of paper I didn't like. Helping other people move out of their houses got me convicted about all my stuff, and I have made some changes in my life.

Now, I have made it a goal to create empty space instead of filling up space. I have one clothes dresser drawer that is empty, one desk drawer at work that is empty; I keep my garage free of junk so my wife can actually park her car there. If I can do it, believe me, you can do it too!

When you decide to dejunk and declutter, it is an ongoing process and up for continual re-evaluation and re-assessment.

Consider

If you are truly ready to get rid of your clutter, I am confident I can help. Here are my mottos, affirmations, and questions that help me think through decluttering and prioritizing my things:

Mottos
- Clutter free is the way to be! (My daughter Amanda came up with that gem!)
- One man's junk is another man's garbage.
- "When in doubt, throw it out!"

Affirmations
- Decluttering is moving things along, not saving, stashing, storing and stacking.
- I am not my stuff.
- My life will not be diminished by throwing out things.
- God is able to supply all my needs! Hanging on to things show a distrust in God and a lack of faith that He is able to supply all my needs in the future.
- Since I have long ago invested money in this item, throwing it out or giving it away is not going to cost me anything. To keep it will cost me time, effort and emotional energy.

Questions
- If I had to do it over, would I purchase this item today?
- If there were a fire, would I risk my life to save this item?
- If I didn't have this item today, would I go out and buy it?
- Does this enrich my life or sap some of the joy from my life?
- Could someone else enjoy or value this as much as I have in the past?
- Have I used this in the past year? Two years? What makes me think I will ever use it?
- Am I willing to admit I will never use all this stuff I'm keeping?

What about Gifts?

If you are afraid of offending someone if you throw a gift out, reexamine your thinking. Remember a few things about gifts given you by someone. First, they might not even remember that they gifted it to you. If they ever do ask about it, you can safely and honestly say that you found someone who really wanted it and re-gifted it to them. They don't have to know that it was the Salvation Army that wanted all your donations.

Get Free

I once thought of having a yard sale but instead I put out some things in front of our home, on a busy street. After a week and the stuff was still there, I thought about putting a price tag on it to see if someone would steal it! The experience underscored the realization that my "valuable" stuff is not so valuable in anyone else's eyes.

So many things that clutter up your lives once seemed valuable.

Now they seem senseless and trivial. It is good to remember that the most important things in life have no monetary value and take up no storage space: they are the things you carry with you in your heart. Besides, things you carry in your heart don't have to be stored and cleaned! There is more help available online if you are serious about changing some hoarding patterns. Getting free from your stuff and creating space in your life will truly free you up to live today as the best day ever.

LIVING THE PLAN

Do you seriously need to think about decluttering and dejunking your possessions? What can you do today to get started?

Can you commit to giving or tossing a bag or box of things away each week until you are clutter free?

What are you passionate about saving and storing? Why do you think you value these items so highly? Imagine what your life would look like if a tornado took all of these possessions away. How would your life be different? Could life go on?

My wife and I were given some "collectable" plates that we were going to sell on-line. Then I learned of a church youth group that was having a yard sale with proceeds going to their camp fund. We donated the plates to the group and they found a person who was interested in purchasing them at a discount. It was a Win-Win. Do you know of a person or group that would be interested in taking some of your stuff off your hands? Box up your items and label them, sealing the lids until you can make arrangements to have them pick it up or you can take it to them. Resist the urge to take just one item out of the box!

12.

NO REGRETS

"...But one thing I do: forgetting what is behind and straining toward what is ahead, I press on toward the goal..."
The Apostle Paul, letter to the Philippians

"I made the wrong choice; I didn't finish college."

"I should have done that."

"I should have married what's his name."

"I shouldn't have done that."

I should have, I shouldn't have, I should have.

Carrying around a boatload of regret and remorse is a way of life for some people. Carrying around a bag of regrets can be a coping strategy for dealing with the reality of every day life. But, is it really the best choice?

Life is too short to have regrets. Carrying regrets is like putting on weights each and every morning and then trying to get through your day encumbered by the extra weight. Regrets cause you to use unnecessary energy just in normal activities.

Yes, regret can be comfortable. When you live with past regrets and remorse, you are in familiar territory. If confronted with the option to change your future or to settle back into the problems you see in your life, will you choose to continue the familiar and more comfortable way of life? Even if what you're currently experiencing is harmful and hurtful?

Living under the pressure of past regret is really a selfish way to live life, if you look at it closely. People cocoon into a protective layer of regrets for events long gone, or for choices made in the past. Regretting the past, dwelling on the negative, second guessing old decisions are simply a waste of energy. It is sad that many people put so much time and energy into lamenting the past instead of reframing the future.

No one that you know of can go back in time and redo the events of the past. However, **many of your lifelong regrets can be restored or remedied with a proactive plan for the future.** You can learn from your past mistakes or misjudgments and create a new chapter for your lives. Friendships and relationships can often be restored, degrees can be earned and jobs can be secured. Do you want to do the hard work of restoration and stop living with regret?

In creating a life without regrets, think on these things:

- *You cannot go back and redo events,* circumstances or choices made in the past. Those things are in the past and untouchable.
- *All you have is this moment.* You cannot deal with the future, except that how you decide to live today will have an impact on your future. You must fully realize

that life is lived in the moment and living with regrets is like mortgaging your future on your past mistakes.

- *You must choose to decide to live without regrets.*
- *You can only change yourself.* You do not have permission to change another person. It is hard enough trying to change your own patterns of thinking and acting. (t takes one person to forgive; it takes two to be reconciled. Sometimes you get to a point where you are ready to reconcile, but the other person may be at a decidedly different place in their life.
- *Enact change.* Make a distinction between the things you can change and those things you cannot change.

The one thing you can change is how you think, feel and act about the events of your past. You can reframe your past. Just like an oil painting can be enhanced by a nice picture frame, so the events of your past can be reframed. Often you can't change the picture but you can change the frame, you can choose how you think about the picture. Sometimes it helps to have a professional counselor help us walk through some of the issues of the past. Sometimes, a good friend who truly listens can make all the difference.

You need to be able to give yourselves the permission to reframe the picture. If you are old enough to be reading these words, **you are mature enough to realize that you hold the keys to your own mental health and growth.** You may have had something terrible happen to you as a child and often you will frame that picture with your childlike understanding. Usually, at these times, you become stunted, mentally. This is where a professional can really help you process your understanding and get you out of places where you feel "stuck."

For those areas where you have some control, you should be ready to do the hard work of rectifying the past, getting the degree or whatever it may be. I am not advocating divorcing your spouse and marrying what's his name, but I am suggesting that you can decide, and you have the power, to make life-altering changes. You can start those changes by what you decide to do today with your past regrets.

This chapter opened with a quote from the Apostle Paul. He had a lot in his past to regret. He was present at the stoning of the first martyr, Steven, and went on to viciously persecute Christians. But Paul gives us insight into his thinking, and how you can deal with the regret of your past, as well: *"...But one thing I do: forgetting what is behind and straining toward what is ahead, I press on toward the goal..."*

Paul has a single focus: "This one thing." In stating, "forgetting what is behind," Paul is not saying that he completely forgot what he did, elsewhere he actually gives a rather thorough list. He is not forgetting, but he is not going to carry the weight of the past. He is putting off the weight because it is in the past. He is passionate and resolved to not dwell on the past. Then, he uses the words, "straining toward what is ahead," and "pressing on toward the goal." These are not the words of a person dwelling on their past mistakes.

These are the words of a champion, a very healthy person who lives fully in the moment unencumbered with the weight of the past. The Apostle Paul accepted his past, dealt with his past. Then in the present, he moved toward the future goal. This is a wonderful model for all of us who need to release the sins, failures and mistakes of the past.

If you need help in resolving the past, please get the help you need from a professional counselor or minister. If you feel you know what needs to be done, and it is something that is in your power to do, and it is the right thing to do, then by all means do what needs to be done. Take your own future by the horns and decide today to deal with the past finally and forever.

For those regrets you can't change or do anything about, well, those can't be changed no matter how much you think about them can they? Why do you still beat yourself up and carry your burdens when you should just lay them down?

> *There is a story of two celibate monks who were of an order that they should not touch women. As the two were walking, they came to a stream and a woman was standing there wondering how to get across. She asked the monks if they would kindly carry her across the stream. One monk stepped forward and picked the woman up and carried her across. On the other side she was very thankful and even offered them money, which they refused. As the two monks continued down the path, it was obvious that the one monk who did not touch the woman was very upset with his brother. Finally he started to speak and he started ranting on how wrong and terrible it was to help the young lady. After he had finished his tirade, the other monk replied, "I am sorry for how you choose to feel, but my brother, I set the woman down miles ago and you are still carrying her!"*

You do not have to live with regrets. You can and should move on. Dwelling on the past today will not solve or change the past, it will only mortgage a happy future. It takes energy to keep holding regrets, grudges and unforgiveness. Let go, give yourself permission to let it go. It is over, learn from it, don't forget it, remember what you have learned from it and grow forward.

Regrets are like huge weights on your legs that will keep you from running today's race. You have the freedom and power to remove the regrets, to take off the weights and see your day today as the best day ever.

LIVING THE PLAN

Practical Steps:
1. Decide that today you will not live with regrets.
2. Decide what action steps need to be taken with any unfinished items from the past.
3. Decide when you are going to do the action steps and resolve to do them.
4. Make today the best day ever free from a life of regrets.

What regrets do you carry with you?

Do you know people who live in the past? Do you find their lives fulfilling and exciting?

Have you been dwelling on events that are out of your control? What else could you do?

What events do you need to "reframe" from your past?

13.

WHAT IS THE WORST THAT CAN HAPPEN?

"And you know that all things work together for good..."
Romans 8:28

In order to make today the best day of your life, you must be ready to mentally meet the challenges of life. If you are fully living this philosophy, life will bring many positive and wonderful events, people and things your way. But life also has a way of throwing us some curve balls. Not adversarial, like a baseball game where the pitcher is trying to get you out, but there are times that you encounter very negative people and circumstances. How are you to respond to these people and events?

Many people living today simply react to circumstances. Their lives are a reaction to everything that goes on during the day. They are not particularly proactive about their day, they just live from event to event with no thought of proactively creating the events or deciding ahead of time what they will do when a particular situation arises. These people are, "living under the circumstances."

Have you ever heard that response? How are you doing? "Well, okay, under the circumstances." My usual reply to that response is, "Why are you choosing to live under the circumstances?" Honestly, doesn't it just make more sense to live above your circumstances? **And, when you think about it, many of those circumstances are really self-imposed, the result of natural consequences for the actions and behaviors you choose.**

At other times, there is no connection between what you are doing or have done and the events that come your way. There is not always a direct cause and effect. In fact, from time to time, bad things do happen to good people. This is inevitable and a part of life. Jesus put it this way; "He [God] makes the sun to shine on the evil and the good and sends rain on the just and the unjust," Matthew 5:45. You don't need to always be terribly introspective and ask, "Why is this happening to me?" **Sometimes, well, stuff just happens.**

When something comes into your life that appears on the surface to be a bad circumstance or event, you still have the power to decide how you will think about and process what is happening. **You always have options.** When you think there are no alternatives, you may get depressed, but there are always options. You, alone, get to decide how you will respond to your circumstances. You can choose to reframe the incident and see it from a different perspective.

Sometimes it is helpful to ask yourself, "What is the worst that can happen?" or "What is the worst that could have happened?" When you understand the incident that just happened to you is not the worst that might have happened, you give yourselves some breathing room to deal with the experience that is in front of you.

Recently, my daughter drove my car to pick my wife and me up from the airport. Before she was out of the driveway, she had a minor accident. My nice car had a dent, but she wasn't hurt. When I realized that it could have been much worse, that my daughter could have been hurt or the car really messed up it helped frame the event into a manageable situation. I had the choice of how I would think about what happened. I was not upset or angry, in fact I was very grateful that it was not as bad as it could have been.

Worst Case Scenario

When you first ask yourself, "What is the worst that can happen?" you begin to weigh your options. When you can accept the worst-case scenario you then can proceed to improve the situation. You may realize that even if the worst thing happened you would still have choices and options. How many times have you heard others, or yourself say, "I didn't have any other option"? The truth is you always have options and some are better than others.

Dale Carnegie said, "Happiness doesn't depend on any external conditions, it is governed by your mental attitude." It is not the circumstance that can get to you; it is how you think about the circumstance. And you have choices, the freedom to think as you please about the things that come into your lives.

> *A friend of mine told me part of his family's story: About a hundred years ago, a relative eagerly awaited the arrival of her daughter and granddaughter, sailing all the way from England. The daughter, being her usual self, arrived late and*

literally missed the boat that day. But, that day, her tardiness saved their lives. The boat they missed was the Titanic. The daughter did not inform her mother who was waiting in America. Upon hearing of the sinking of the ship, and of all the people who lost their lives, the mother assumed the worst and died of a broken heart.

Her daughter and granddaughter didn't die; she believed they died. It is not the circumstance it is what you believe about the situation that will influence your behavior.

Lets put this idea to rest once and for all. No matter what happens in your life you are able to deal with it and you will get through it. Tragic things have happened to people but they have gotten through it. So will you. Regardless of your circumstances, events or situations, these do not need to keep you from having the best day ever. The choice is up to you.

Best Case Scenario

You have seen how thinking the worst case scenario can actually help frame your current reality in a positive way by giving us the opportunity to consider your options and realize you have choices. Now let's consider how thinking about the best case scenario can help us realize a preferred future, one to your own making and liking. Why is it so difficult for some people to think, "What is the best thing that could happen to me today?"

Do you need some practice in being more positively proactive with your day? Think about this, what if I told you that today you had won a million dollar lottery? How would that make you feel? Take a moment and let that feeling or emotion sink in.

Would winning that much money make you happy? Is there a sort of euphoria that would come from such good news? Now, what creates the happiness, the money or the news? You don't possess the money; the only thing that has changed is what you believe happened. Winning the money is a very positive sensation and wonderful news, but nothing has really changed with your situation. Only your perception of what has happened has changed, your attitude shifted. That same anticipation can be applied each and every new day as you and I anticipate the joy of the new day and all it will bring.

Choose today how you will think and how you process the news of the day. Carnegie also said: "It isn't what you have, or who you are, or where you are, or what you are doing that makes you happy or unhappy. It is what you think about." Thinking makes it so.

What you may really fear in a crisis is loosing control. When you have the emotional strength to realize that you have options and choices you do not need to fear the loss of control. You cannot actually control every event, but you do have the power to control how you frame events, and how you will think about those events.

It is tremendously empowering to realize that no matter what happens, you are in control of your own thinking and you have the choice to decide how you will respond.

Choose today to make this day the very best day of your life.

LIVING THE PLAN

An affirmation to remember:

> *I choose to be happy, at peace and content today regardless of my circumstances.*

Have you ever had an experience that was so tragic you thought you would not get through it? How did you cope with it?

Consider an event you are facing in your life right now. Project the idea of the worst case scenario into that event. What would that look like? How would you respond to the worst case? Can you see how this activity frees you up to consider options that you may not have seen earlier? What new options or choices have opened up to you regarding that situation?

Yesterday in Washington, a woman who thought she won a $40,000 lottery was informed that the figure was 4 million. Imagine what she thought and experienced. What would you do with an additional 4 million dollars? Just for today, why don't you keep the idea in your mind that you have this extra money. Notice how you feel and how you respond to this day's events.

14.

YOUR OWN WORST ENEMY

"As a man thinks in his heart, so is he."
Proverbs 23:7

Have you ever said something that you wish you hadn't? You may have heard, "Out of the heart the mouth speaks." What is on the inside usually works its way to the outside. Your heart attitude comes out in your words.

You really are your own worst enemy. Sabotage, feelings of low self worth, believing negative input from family and friends, people putting others down in order to get ahead, these are all seeds of your own destruction. If you watch any television you come to the conclusion that the world thrives on sarcasm and negative put downs and the disrespect of others. However, negative put downs, sarcasm, and disrespect have no place in your life. You certainly don't want to be treated that way and you should not want to treat others that way, either.

Another self-defeating behavior is the problem of expectations. You want things to work out to your satisfaction, and when they don't you resort to all sorts of unpleasant behaviors and pathologies. You become bitter, angry and lead a life of unforgiveness.

If it is true that you are your own worst enemy, that the seeds of your own destruction are in your own life, then the inverse must also be true that you are your own best friend. The seeds of your success are within you not outside of you. Many people seek fulfillment outside of themselves, in things, titles, money etc. These external things are the counters used to compute self worth and a scorecard to determine where a person is on the scale of things. Yet, these things are not accurate measures of your self-worth.

This all comes back to personal responsibility. Who decides for you what kind of day you will have? You do. Yet, you may at some point tend to submarine your days, holding back, not going full throttle, not believing that today can become the best day of your life.

Have you ever seen this played out in your life? Blaming others and not taking responsibility for your actions? How have you ever found yourself holding back? Today, you have permission to break out and be free! Hold nothing back, save no energy in reserve for a "later" that never comes.

Negative self-talk sometimes focuses on the behaviors and actions of others. You prove in your mind that other people are the problem. Your poor self-image has you defeated before you begin. I know a woman with poor self-esteem who blames everyone else for her situation in life. If you are around here very long, you become one of her excuses! (We will discuss more about toxic people in chapter 18.)

There are voices in your head, sometimes put there by people who were once important and significant to you; teachers, parents, older siblings and friends. You buy into these voices and believe them, even if they have no basis in reality. Your mind tells you that these people must be experts on you because they are so important, and you end up believing what these people say about you.

It takes work to weed your mental garden and get rid of the crab grass and noxious weeds that take root. Others may have planted these unwanted thoughts or you could have cultivated them yourself. Once you recognize these voices, or weeds, you can also plant the seeds of success in your life. Where once you may have planted the seeds of failure or nurtured the opinions of others you can now choose to plant your own ideas.

Imagine you are at a garden store or nursery. You are looking at the rack of seeds labeled; "Seeds of Self-Destruction." Notice the names on each package:

- Sarcasm
- Putting people down
- Lack of self-esteem and respect
- Negative self-talk
- Blaming others
- Living in the past with regrets
- Believing the opinions, and feelings of others toward you
- Abusing substances

Do these sound like items you would want to plant in the garden of your soul? They are the seeds of self destructive, self-defeating and self-sabotaging behaviors.

You are the gardener of your soul. You truly do become what you think about, what you nurture in your mental garden. The choice is yours, to have a happy, healthy garden full of life and good fruit or a garden of weeds, harmful grass and vines. Sometimes the unwanted and toxic weeds are placed in your garden by others, but it is your responsibility, your garden, and you must pull out those invasive plants and allow the good vegetation to grow.

If you are not careful you can end up shooting yourself in the foot. You may live with regrets, regretting missed opportunities in the past and fearing that the future will not be any better. Your negative self-talk includes things like: "I should have finished college, I should have... I should not have..." You end up beating yourself up from the inside. The game is lost in the head before it is ever lost on the court. You can either choose to anticipate failure or success; the choice is up to you!

LIVING THE PLAN

If someone who knew you wrote about you, someone who knew you as well as you know yourself, what words would they use to describe you? What stories would they tell which reveal who you really are?

Can you identify with some of the self-defeating behaviors in this chapter? Which ones?

What do you think would help you overcome these self-defeating behaviors? Make a list of possible solutions and choose one in which to try or experiment with.

What is growing in the garden of your soul?

What do you wish to cultivate in your soul's garden?

15.

SELF-IMPOSED LIMITATIONS

"I can do all things through Christ who strengthens me."
Philippians 4:13

You have heard the epic stories of individuals with physical impairments or disabilities doing great things, pushing through and destroying obstacles that hold back ordinary people, the Helen Keller's of the world who do not consider their disability as an excuse to fail but a challenge to overcome. The blind man that climbs Mt. Everest and the marine with no legs running a marathon in record time are both examples of people who do not let their disability define what they can accomplish. These overcomers put many of us to shame as we compare our own small pursuits and lukewarm performances.

In the movie "Chicken Run," Ginger, the lead chicken trying to get everyone out of the chicken farm safely, warns her other chickens, "The fences are not out there, they are in your heads." Truly the limitations you find, the boundaries around you, are often self-imposed. The obstacles you encounter in the physical world are first encountered in your mind. Even choosing words like; "obstacle" or "problem" rather than using empowering words like "challenge" and "opportunity" demonstrate the root of self-inflicted limitations.

When you face a challenge you look at the situation from your past experiences, flipping through the file cabinet in your minds to see if this has happened to us before. As you open the file on that situation, alternatives are reviewed and based on past experiences you choose a course of action which you hope will be successful. You build up a litany of experiences. When you encounter a similar experience you review the old files which you have created in the past, categorizing the new situation with similar situations of your past.

Have you ever heard someone say, "Oh, I'm not mechanical," or, "I can't swim," "I don't want to go to the dentist," "I don't remember names well." I don't I don't I don't... You are building a life, one decision at a time. Over time, you come to rely on past decisions, (the file cabinet) this is when you either decide to overcome or yield to your own self imposed limitations.

Who said you can't draw, for example? You said it, "I can only draw stick figures." Where does this self talk, this self imposed limitation come from? Quite likely, it comes from public school, teachers and other students who laughed at your pictures. Perhaps, it was a parent who did not put your drawing on the refrigerator and you later found it in the garbage. You filed these experiences carefully in your mental file cabinet. You might have even labeled the file, "Artistic Ability."

When you let others shape you and tell you what you can and cannot do, you are believing a lie. Afterwards, you begin to tell yourself the lie, over and over, again. Maybe you even hear a voice, clearly and distinctly, possibly the third grade teacher saying, "You will never be good at drawing." Whatever the source, you internalize other's values and estimates of your abilities and then you work to insure the truth of what you believe, what you have imprinted on your minds.

Who is it you are listening to when you hear this restrictive self-talk? You need to have child like faith, simple, no boundaries, children don't intuitively know boundaries, they believe they can do anything they want, including jumping off a roof and flying like Superman.

It begins with the mind and how you think about something. **What you say to yourself in your mind causes you to work overtime to help you become the person you imagine yourself to be.** You either win or loose at the outset, even before you pick up the pencil to draw or whatever you do. Using the analogy of the file cabinet, you go and look for similar experiences to the one you are facing and you normally won't even attempt the project or experience.

Here is a rather revealing and tough question:

What would you attempt to do if you knew for certain you would not fail?

It tried this out in my life. I asked myself the question, "What would you attempt to do if you knew for certain you would not fail?" I have a family of artists and they can draw anything or paint beautifully. (Last year my son did a painting in 20 minutes and it sold for $15,000!) My internal file said I could neither draw or paint, so I decided to shut the file and begin to draw and paint.

Admittedly, at the beginning, I was rather sophomoric, all right, I wasn't very good, but I enjoyed the process more than the product and I gave myself the permission to learn and grow into an artist. There have been many learnings along the way, such as the fact that everyone does art differently. No two people can paint alike. You are as different and as unique as your fingerprints.

As I write these words, I am preparing for my first gallery show and I anticipate having one of my larger works hanging in a corporate office building very soon. My artwork is unique, and it is not for everyone, but finally I have broken the chains of my self-imposed limitations and am free to pursue my creativity through art.

The question in front of you begins with success instead of failure. It puts the mind in a state of anticipation. Instead of looking through the mental file cabinet to see if you are going to win or loose, you anticipate the success at the start. Maybe this is why kids are so ready to try anything. They don't have flies and files of people telling them they can't do something and the experience to back it up. They anticipate at the outset that they can do anything.

You can do anything, especially make today the best day of your life.

LIVING THE PLAN

What would you attempt to do today if you knew you could not fail?

16.

EXPECTATIONS VS. EXPECTANCY

"Faith is the substance of things hoped for, the evidence of things not seen."
Hebrews 11:1

When Molly (not her real name) came into my office she was literally a basket case. She sobbed as she told me her story. I had heard a similar story many times over the years, but each time, only the cast of characters were different.

Nothing was working out as Molly had planned. Her husband, her kids, her employer and workmates, and even her friends had all disappointed her. "What is wrong with me?" Molly asked. "I am anxious and tied up in knots." "Why does nothing work out like I plan? Why can't people do what they are supposed to do?"

After I let Molly finish her half hour, "poor me" story it was my turn. I asked her some leading questions and tried to focus the conversation. I suggested she choose one situation and we could walk through that together. She said something that was hurting her recently was that her husband did not buy her the earrings she wanted for her birthday.

"Did he know you wanted the earrings?" I asked.

"Yes, we saw them in the mall a couple of weeks before my birthday."

"Did you tell him specifically that you wanted the earrings for your birthday?"

"No, but he should have known by how I was admiring them."

"Did you remind him about the earrings?"

"Of course not, then it would not be from his heart. He should have remembered. Instead he bought me a hideous dress. It was all I could do to keep from crying—and this was my birthday!"

I shared with Molly that there is a big difference between the words expectation and expectancy. Expectancy "faiths" the future rather than just trying to bravely face the future. Expectancy neutralizes the anxiety of expectations by allowing you to believe in the grace and goodness of our God, freely accepting and being grateful for the events and situations that sovereignly come into your life. When you release your need for control and manipulation, you can rest in the quiet assurance that God is working all things together for your good.

When you live in the sphere of expectations, you are expecting others to perform to your, well, expectations. This is a formula for failure and discouragement. You are actually giving others the power to control how you feel. You must not force your expectations on other people, events or circumstances. You should not give any person or thing the power to influence your peace and joy.

Whether you tend to live your life with either expectations or expectancy makes all the difference in the world! Those, like Molly, who live with expectations are defeated at the beginning. No one will ever live up to your expectations. **You can't even live up to the expectations you have for yourself, let alone others.** When you live your life with expectations, you are often let down and confused. You are setting yourself up for anxiety and trouble. You are disappointed, and can even get to the point where you question God's goodness in your life.

Christmas and family events can be wonderful for people living in expectancy, but are especially difficult for people who live with expectations. At Christmastime and throughout the year, those who have expectations will be expecting what gifts they will receive, what will happen to them, how family members and others will treat them, etc... Expectancy, on the other hand, frees you up to accept the new things that flow into and out of your life. When you live your life with the attitude of expectancy and anticipation, you will see a big change in your own behavior and the behaviors and actions of others.

Do you tend to live with expectations or in expectancy?

EXPECTATION	EXPECTANCY
Has a preconceived way something "should" happen	Patiently waiting to see what will happen
Anxious- Worrying about future	Faithing and trust in God for Successful outcomes
Seeing IS believing	Believing IS seeing
Insists on my own way	Submits to God's design
Sad when the situation does not work out in my preconceived way	Happy and contented in the outcomes knowing God works all thing together for my good.
Me—mine, wanting power and control	Ours—yours finding strength in serving

You have a choice today to live with expectations or expectancy. **Expectations will seldom match reality,** people will let us down and you will be anxious and prone to worry. You might also try to force people to meet your expectations through various dysfunctional methods, such as: intimidation, guilt, anger, triangulation, gossip and a variety of other behaviors.

However, when you live each day in joyful expectancy and anticipation, you live a fuller, freer life. You are also a lot more fun to be around when you are not trying to control people and events.

After Molly and I talked for awhile, I asked her what would have happened if she had not had any expectation for her husband or her birthday, but instead waited in anticipation for whatever would take place? Molly confided somewhat sheepishly that her husband's choice of a dress was really not that bad, and in fact he had planned a whole evening together on her birthday, and she had a bad attitude all night. It spoiled everything, but up till now, she thought it was all his fault. She had torpedoed her own birthday by her insistence on her expectations being met.

Resolve to make this the best day of your life. Give up your expectations and substitute those expectations for expectancy. Be thankful for what comes into your life today and don't try to control or force the outcomes.

This day will be the best ever! You don't need to force it or have positive expectations. You simply have to live out your values through your character and expectantly wait to see how this day will unfold into the best day of your life so far!

Here are some good memory verses to help you have a sense of expectancy for what God will do through all the events in your life:

"...casting all your anxiety on Him, because He cares for you."
I Peter 5:7 NASB

"No, dear brothers and sisters, I have not achieved it, but I focus on this one thing: Forgetting the past and looking forward to what lies ahead, I press on to reach the end of the race and receive the heavenly prize for which God, through Christ Jesus, is calling us." Philippians 3:13-14 NLT

"...but they who wait for the LORD shall renew their strength; they shall mount up with wings like eagles; they shall run and not be weary; they shall walk and not faint." Isaiah 40:31 ESV

"'Bring the whole tithe into the storehouse, so that there may be food in My house, and test Me now in this,' says the LORD of hosts, 'if I will not open for you the windows of heaven and pour out for you a blessing until it overflows.'" Malachi 3:10 NASB

LIVING THE PLAN

Identify those places, times or people with which you have expectations. Compare your item or list with the chart in this chapter. Notice how having expectancy rather than expectations, can help the situation.

Do you agree with the statement that when you live with expectations you give others the power to influence and control you? Why or why not?

Choose a situation where you are anxious or tend to worry. Think through the points in this chapter with that situation in mind. Notice the difference expectations and expectancy bring to the situation. Put together a list of possible outcomes for either side, and decide what action steps you will take.

17.

SETTING BOUNDARIES

"As much as possible, live in peace with all men."
Romans 12:18

There are boundaries in healthy relationships. Someone said, "Good fences make good neighbors." So it is with relationships; you have to know where the boundaries are, where the fences are. In the book, "Real Simple Parenting," Janis Hanson and my wife, Susan, co-wrote about teaching your children the boundaries. They said it is important to first instruct before there is correction. Many people will correct or discipline their children before they have clearly defined the boundaries. Unmet expectations bring frustration. When you encounter people who have preconceived expectations for your behavior, you need to kindly but clearly communicate your boundaries.

Boundary setting is letting other people know how you want to be treated and how you will treat them. It is important to set and maintain boundaries with people, but especially the toxic or very needy persons. These people can quickly drain your energy!

Here then, is my definition of a boundary: "Boundaries are the rules, limits, guidelines and consequences that a person initiates in their own life to communicate with others what is reasonable, safe, permissible and acceptable ways of treating one another." **You cannot have a healthy meaningful relationship with someone who will not respect your boundaries.** Personal boundaries identify you as an individual, spelling out your likes and dislikes, and setting the perimeters you will accept in your life.

Boundaries show:

- Self-control
- Responsibility for your thoughts, words, attitudes, and actions
- Love and care for others and yourself

Boundaries are not:

- *Manipulating, or controlling, others.* Good boundaries are not about manipulation or controlling others. It is about self-control and self-acceptance. you will certainly be accused of attempting to control people when you set boundaries, but it is not about controlling the other person, it is communicating the way you wish to be treated and holding people accountable to what you view as acceptable. Other people have a choice how they will respond to your boundaries and that is up to them.
- *Avoiding responsibility.* Setting boundaries is one of the keys to accepting responsibility for yourselves and your lives. You are not avoiding taking responsibility, you are actually taking responsibility for the things which you

have control over—yourself.

- *Making threats.* Good boundaries are not about threatening, embarrassing, cajoling, manipulating, or "guilting" people. You may set boundaries based off of other people's decisions and behaviors.

In order to experience today as the best day of your life, it is necessary to have healthy boundaries with others. Boundaries show respect and trust, both of these ingredients are necessary for a healthy relationship. The very definition of a poor relationship is one without mutual respect and trust. Healthy relationships are also able to speak truth in love, to communicate.

One day, a woman walked into my office and told me that she was going to get a divorce. I asked her if her husband had been unfaithful or abusive and she said no. I asked her why she was so set on getting a divorce and she replied, "God wants me to be happy, my husband does not make me happy, so I am getting a divorce."

I told her that she had two misconceptions. The first was that God wanted her to be happy. I explained that God is looking for obedient children and that there is joy when you serve Him obediently according to His word. The second misconception is that it is up to her husband to make her happy. I shared that happiness was her choice, and not the result of other's behaviors. No person can make us happy; it is always your choice to be happy or unhappy.

She really did not like to hear what I had to say and so she left my office and before slamming the door said, "If you don't support me in this divorce, you can't be my friend anymore." She was not creating a boundary as much as she was threatening me. Obviously, I could not support such a capricious reason for a divorce and it was also obvious that I was not going to perform to her expectations. That was the last "conversation" we ever had.

So that you don't think it is only women who do this sort of thing, a former Marine was upset with a decision I made. Rather than talking with me about it, he stuck his face in my office door and said, "Don't ever talk to me again, you are not my friend." I knew he was in no mood to talk so I simply said, "Well you are still my brother and I love you in the LORD." He spat back to me, "You are not MY brother!" and with that also slammed my door. (My poor door gets the brunt of it!)

I thought it ironic that this man who prides himself as a former marine would forget the Corps motto, Semper Fi: "Always Faithful." Apparently he would be faithful to me as the leader, as long as I performed to his unspoken expectations.

In the two dramatic examples I have shared, there were some narcissistic tendencies at work. The narcissist does not recognize boundaries, other people simply exist to meet the need of the narcissist or they might as well not exist at all. These are extreme cases and thankfully not the usual situation.

You will see how empowering setting boundaries is in your life. Setting boundaries shows that you are a friend to yourselves and helps you discover true friendship in others. Those who do not respect your boundaries are the ones who manipulate, abuse, cast shame, betray, are two faced and will eventually abandon you, and should be avoided until they are willing to accept you and your boundaries.

Setting boundaries can help you recognize those who are true friends, people you can communicate with, and honor boundaries that you set. Being able to give and take, to set boundaries and request that you be treated with respect and honor, takes skill for us to communicate directly and honestly. It is truth in love.

You must treat others with love and respect because you value the image of God in others and because you are commanded by your Lord to exhibit unconditional love for each other.

John Gottman in his "Love Lab" at the University of Washington discovered the connection between how long a married couple would stay married based on their patterns of communication. What is said is as important as how it is said. Your communication establishes the framework for successful boundary setting.

You cannot have a healthy meaningful life if you do not set personal boundaries and hold people to them. This is also considered, "self care" the ability to make sure you are healthy and functional, not neglecting or putting yourself down, but being a true friend to yourself. You really can't help others if you are personally drained and depleted.

For more information on setting boundaries, I recommend the "Boundaries" books and workbooks by Cloud and Townsend.

LIVING THE PLAN

How can the "disease to please" get us into trouble?

Do you find it difficult to stand up for yourself sometimes? Do you often find yourself agreeing to do things you really didn't want to do? Do you avoid conflict with pushy selfish people? Do you end up taking things personally?

What are some boundaries you need to set immediately?

18.

PERSONAL TRANSFORMATION

" And be not conformed to this world but be transformed
by the renewing of your mind..."
Romans 12:2

For some of us, this idea of making today the best day of our lives is a real paradigm shift. My own journey with this great concept has taken many years to internalize, process and implement. Gandhi said that you must be the change you seek. More and more I understand his wisdom and insight into personal transformation.

Some people call this process renewal, reprogramming or personal transformation. It is the process of reinventing yourself and reprogramming your mind for success. As you grow, you experience personal transformation. In fact, all growth is transformation.

There is a wonderful model of this concept that can be seen in nature: The caterpillar that transforms into a butterfly. From crawling on the ground to fluttering through the flowers in flight, this is one truly amazing transformation, yet the change in your own life can be just as dramatic. This renewal is about change and it is change for good.

The caterpillar goes through several stages of transformation: from the caterpillar state to the Chrysalis state and finally to the Butterfly. What we may overlook is the long gestation period, or the time of processing and doing the work necessary to launch a successful butterfly.

We all go through these stages when we seek personal transformation. How much time you spend in each phase is individually determined. In one theory of change making, first introduced by James Prochaska and Carlo DiClemente in the 1970's, proposed a process of change making with 6 stages.

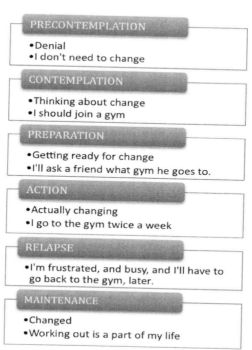

No one can make another person go through these stages of personal transformation, because people must ultimately change themselves. And you only change when you are ready to do the work necessary for the change. Some people visit the gym for years and never loose a pound because they have not changed their eating habits or sedentary lifestyle. They are only kidding themselves that going to the gym will result in the lasting change they seek.

I get wary of programs that promise immediate results. These are often short-lived and rarely reach the stage of a life change or maintenance. I have actually become immune to advertizing that offers the quick fix or a set period of time, such as eight weeks to your ideal weight, or whatever. It is not a short term change, but a change for life. Change for good is long-term: It is a lifestyle change.

The Mind at Work

So it is with changing how you think about the world, about each day and your place in it. Your mind is a wonderful tool. Knowing how the mind works can help you process your ideas and can turn your life around. When you change your thinking you change your life and how you interact with your world.

Your mind works at conscious and subconscious levels. On the conscious level, you can think one thought at a time. There are those people who can switch quickly between thoughts or ideas and appear to be "multi-tasking" but in reality the mind can only entertain one thought at a time.

On a subconscious level, your mind is constantly working. You are taking in hundreds of inputs, sights, sounds and smells and filtering out what is useful and sending up to the conscious level, those things that it deems important.

Who determines what is important? You do. You program your subconscious mind to decide which information, impressions, etc. it sends into your conscious thought control center. As the conscious mind can only entertain one thought at a time, the one your mind deems as most important is the one that takes priority.

If you are crossing the street and you see something on the other side that attracts your immediate attention, and you focus on that item, suddenly you see a car moving quickly toward you. You quickly determine what the safest thing would be at the moment. Your mind is interrupting your current stream of thought with a more important issue that takes priority: your safety.

In the morning, your subconscious has been busy all night long. You do not have to get up and process a lot of information. You have been "sleeping on it" all night. You do not have to wake up and think, "Do I like Broccoli?" "For which team am I a fan?" "How do I get to work?" "What is my mother's name?" All these things and much, much more are stored in your long-term memory. This huge amount of information can be accessed by your conscious or subconscious mind at any time.

You may be at a buffet filling your plate. As you look at all the food, you want certain items and you skip over other things. Some of the food may actually make you feel sick as you look at it, because you had a similar dish and it did make you sick and your subconscious is remembering that for you.

Reprogramming

Yes, your mind is amazing. It can be programmed to help you meet your life's goals or you can just put it on autopilot and go through your life not thinking about thinking. You can be in the Precontemplation phase and blissfully unaware that you need to change your thinking patterns. This powerful tool, your mind, can change your life if you change your thinking.

You have an awesome opportunity to transform your thinking, to literally reprogram your mind. Once your mind is programmed, your brain helps you do and think in the way you've programmed it. You are in control of the programming of your own mind, and you are responsible for the outcomes, as well.

The subconscious voice has the ability to break into your conscious thinking and remind you of the programming. You tell yourself what you have lead your mind to believe is the truth and what you want out of life. Then, you brain goes to work helping you keep on track with internal voices like, "You shouldn't take that extra piece of cake," "You don't like it when..." and on and on. The internal voices are the programming we have placed there and our brains are very helpful in keeping us to the program of our beliefs.

In any life change there must be personal transformation. This transformation is a simple process but it is not easy. The old programming in our minds must be replaced with the new program and that must be drilled down into our subconscious thinking, not just our conscious thoughts. This is why it is so important to commit good affirmations to memory. When the conscious mind keeps thinking a thought over and over, the subconscious begins to believe the new idea is important and it will filter out the thoughts and experiences of life based on the new information or programming.

Now that we have laid the groundwork for living your best day ever, and we have looked at the roadblocks and setbacks, you are probably ready for the last phase of this book: Living the Life. Thanks for reading this far and may you be empowered in the next and final section.

LIVING THE PLAN

In what area or areas of your life would you like to see personal transformation? What have you done up to now about these areas? What plan can you put into place and implement based on what you have read in this chapter?

Do you recognize and understand the stages of personal transformation as explained in the chapter? See if you are able to share this with another person without notes. If not, go back and reread this chapter until you are able to present and discuss it clearly.

This week, work at listening to your inner voice. Make a list of what your former programming is telling you on a daily basis. Later evaluate this list and write your new programming ideas next to any old ones that you would like to replace.

19.

IT'S YOUR CHOICE

"Choose for yourselves, this day, whom you will serve...
but for me and my house we will serve the Lord."
Joshua 24:15

When someone tells you that you have a choice, does that make you feel uncomfortable? Do you avoid situations where you have to make a decision? There is a facet in the human nature that tends to abdicate responsibility. When a person has to make a choice or comes to a place where a decision must be made, often times the person is concerned not as much with the decision, but the outcome of the decision and whether or not it was a wise decision and what other people will think of their choice.

Many people, when it comes to choice, will simply decide not to choose, which is a decision in and of itself. Procrastinators get their own satisfaction for delaying or putting off making a choice. When you have decided to make this day the best day of your life, this is a choice for which you take complete responsibility.

No one else chooses how you will live your day. Conversely you have no one to blame but yourself, if you don't make the most of this opportunity that you have before us today. Free will, the opportunity to choose, is a gift our Creator gave us, and as an adult you are responsible for the choices in your life. You may not be able to choose all the things that come into your life, but you can choose how those things impact your life. You have the opportunity to reframe bad experiences, to recast, reimagine, recreate. You are in charge of your own choices, your decisions and what you think about those decisions.

Human nature wants to blame others for your circumstances, but if you look deep enough you realize that the mistakes in your lives are primarily the result of your own choices and you need to stop blaming and stop denying and start taking responsibility. You can learn from your mistakes, learn and improve. When you make a mistake and fall, that is not in itself bad, the failure is not to get up after you have fallen. The question really becomes, "How high will you bounce?" Some bosses will give their employees complete freedom to fall on their faces, knowing full well that going through these experiences are some of the richest learning opportunities.

Mistakes are usually not fatal or final. There is something, however, you can learn from them, you need to take responsibility in the way you deal with people. How you get along in life is not defined by what happens to us, but how you respond to those events. You are responsible for the present. You are not responsible for what actually happened to you growing up, but you are responsible for how those experiences shape your life today and the impact what happed to you previously is having in you today.

How you live your life today and the choices you make do not have to be made solely on the basis of the past, you have a choice to recast and reframe those experiences, **you have a choice of how you will act today.**

You can't blame your parents or siblings or any other person for the attitudes and actions you have decided to exhibit after a crisis or even after a life shaping event in your lives.

Bad things do happen to good people, but good people learn and grow from the things that happen to them. They grow in wisdom and knowledge.

There are some real consequences for failing to take responsibility: These become alternative behaviors that somehow the subconscious uses to abdicate responsibility.

- *Anger.* A person might say, "Life has treated me unfairly and I will lash out in anger and hostility."
- *Depression.* Some people cannot make a decision, or they fail to take responsibility, because they are depressed.
- *People Pleasing.* These people want others to recognize and approve and affirm and accept them for who hey are, even though their track record is miserable.
- *Fearful.* Unable to trust themselves in making decisions, frightened of everything that comes into their paths, these people are taken captive in their minds by fear.
- *Chronic Failures.* These people fail in every relationship, enterprise, and pretty much everything they take on in life. There is a message in their mind that they are a complete failure and the act this out time and time again.

- *Unhealthy*. Physically and/or mentally unhealthy. Or, they have an addictive personality, looking to external sources for comfort, these people are typically unable to ever trust or feel secure with others.

There are many different coping mechanisms for failing to take charge of your life. These coping behaviors, these defining behaviors, have names and labels. These describe those who do not take personal responsibility. Names like, looser, quitter, martyr, complainer, stubborn, pessimist, hostile, obstinate, aggressive, irrational passive, insecure, neurotic, guilt ridden, obsessed, troubled and did you notice that none of those words are positive?

In order to make this day the very best of your life, you will need to take personal responsibility, regardless of what comes into your life, you are going to make this day the very best day of your life. You are going to take personal responsibility for your attitudes, and your actions when you need to make a decision or a choice, listen carefully to your inner dialogue, see if there are some old messages from the past, and then let go of the irrational fears and thoughts that you may have. Release any anger, blame and insecurity. Tell yourself the truth and put into your mind positive self-affirmations.

LIVING THE PLAN

No one can force you to think or feel or do something you don't want to do.

Have you ever experienced a failure and then bounced back?

What did you learn from that situation?

How would you explain what it means to fail forward?

Are there areas in your life where you do not wish to take personal responsibility?   What are they?   (If you abdicate responsibility, who ends up being responsible?)

What experiences from your past need to be reframed?   How will you accomplish this task?

20.

GOALS

"I know the plans I have for you...Plans to give you a hope and a future."
Jeremiah 29:11

When you determine that today is going to be the best day of your life, you are taking control of your destiny. You are being responsible. This determination can become a goal you set for yourself. This particular goal takes you from merely making a living to making an exciting life. Whether or not you are into goals, please, read this chapter carefully and then consider what you will do in the area of your own personal goal setting.

Goals are separate from desires. Simply stated, goals are something you are responsible for; desires require the buy-in of others. While that sounds simple, in reality many people get tripped up at this very point. We need to unpack this concept first because it is a critical difference that will make an incredible difference in your life.

When I ask couples in my counseling and coaching sessions,

"What would you like to see happen?" The responses I get are often based on the other person or spouse's performance. For example, "I want him to be more loving and less angry." This could never be a goal, because it does not take into account personal responsibility and it is directly tied to the behavior of another person.

A parent will tell me, "I want my child to (fill in the blank)." The reality, again, is that you cannot make someone else do something. You can create the motivation and discipline to get the job done, but this is still not a goal because it involves the buy-in of another person. We can desire our spouse or child to do something but it can never be a goal.

I am sure you get the idea. Goals are something that we set for ourselves. They are about our performance, skills and choices. Personal goals are ones that don't require the participation of anyone else—just you. Your success depends completely on your own actions and attitude, and you get to decide what the goal will be. You can't make a goal for someone else, or have a goal that requires someone else to perform in some way.

Why Set Goals

What would you like to see happen in your life? Maybe you have sat down at the beginning of a new year and written out some resolutions. For many people the New Year's resolutions are forgotten by March. You may have tried to set some goals for yourself in the past and had some success with that. More often than not, you probably do not meet your goals. One of the problems with both New Year's resolutions and goal setting is that many people go about it making change in the wrong way. They become quickly discouraged, derailed and defeated.

Reasons for Goals

The first reason to set goals is to have clarity with the direction you want to go. You may have heard the quote: "A problem well stated is half solved." When you force yourself to write out your goals, you are clearly stating what you want to see happen. When you write your goals down instead of just keeping them in your head, you further clarify and commit to the desired outcome. You can review your written goals regularly to stay on track and to celebrate successes along the way.

Goals can help you define what you are going to accomplish and what it will take to get you there. You set goals to help you say "yes" to some things and "no" to other things. Sometime, you have to say "no" to some good things, so that the better things can come your way. Goals can give you the definition, the boundaries, the clarity to chart your course.

The second reason to set goals is to help reprogram your mind for transformation. You need all of your faculties working for you if you are to realize your goals. It is vital that you are telling yourself, clearly and concisely, what it is you are attempting to accomplish. When you drill your desired outcome down into your subconscious, your mind works overtime to help you realize your goals. Your mind will look for opportunities to fulfill your goals. It will help you seek out the people, events and places that will get you closer to your desired outcome.

The third reason to set goals is that you are a thousand times more likely to achieve what you desire if you have well-written goals. We have already considered some of the reasons why well written goals are more easily realized, and the strength to accomplish these goals can be multiplied when shared with others. For example, one of the items on my bucket list was climbing a Mayan pyramid. I shared my list with my wife. When my wife was looking to book a cruise for our family, she remembered my goal and found a Caribbean cruise that included a stop in Belize with an optional tour of Mayan pyramids! It was such a thrill to share that experience with my whole family. The thought occurred to me when we were all on top of the highest Mayan pyramid and taking pictures, that if I had not shared this desire with my wife, I would not be sharing this experience with my family.

Another reason to share your well-written goals with others is to hold you accountable for your decisions and actions. If you are doing something that is keeping you from your goals, a well-meaning friend may help you refocus by calling attention to the goal you shared with them. There is something empowering about sharing your goals with friends, your spouse or others who will encourage you and follow your progress or even suggest ways to meet your goals that you did not consider. Also, when you begin to get discouraged with your progress, having someone hold you accountable to your goals may give you courage and passion to stay the course.

Setting Good Goals

You want to set goals that give you the greatest opportunity for success and reaching your desired outcomes. One way to do this is by setting SMART goals. You have probably heard of SMART goals. It is an acrostic for helping remember the steps in setting good goals. The actual words are different when presented by different people, so the acronym can represent many different concepts, but the main idea is the same:

Specific, Measurable (or motivational), Achievable (or accountable; attainable), Relevant (or responsible; realistic),

Time-Based (or timely; time-bound; touchable). There are also many other words to describe the SMART goal idea. Of course, all of these concepts point to the fact that it is smart to set goals. When you set realistic goals, you are a step closer in accomplishing your goal.

Specific. This is a goal statement, and should be a short paragraph of one or two sentences describing the goal or desired outcome.

Measurable. This is a description of how to measure the goal; how can you tell when the goal is accomplished?

Achievable. This part is critical; goals must be realistic and attainable in order for us to put our whole heart into them.

Relevant. How is this goal important to you and why? When you have a strong enough "Why" you will find the "How to." You also need to know what benefits will come if you reach the goal.

Timely. This is the section where you lay out your time line - there should be a definite start and end date and any milestones should have clearly defined parameters.

There is a marked difference between achievement and success. Achievement is the daily working toward a worthy goal, success is attaining that desired goal outcome. If you break your goals down into workable, manageable sections or steps, you can work toward achieving each step until you reach the final destination. Celebrating achievement along the way may keep you motivated while success is still in the future. When you truly live one day at a time, your best day ever, then you should be grateful for the daily accomplishments you see as you work toward your worthy chosen goals.

If you are to really see today become the best day of your life, you must live with the realization that you do not accomplish your goals in a day. Remember, anything of value takes work and takes time; however, if you are on a continuum toward reaching your goal, then each day you can celebrate the achievement toward that successful outcome.

SMART Goals are Specific

Specific goals are much more likely to be accomplished than vague ones! A specific goal can be determined by asking the following questions:

- WHO is involved? Smart goals don't depend on the involvement of too many people. Remember, the only person you can control is yourself, so the achievement of your goal should depend on you.
- WHAT do you want to accomplish? Define your aim, so you have a clear idea of what you are aiming for. A vague, "I want to be a better person," is not specific enough!
- WHERE will you work on your goal? Identify a location or locations where most of the work towards your goal will be carried out.
- WHEN do you hope to accomplish your goal? Set a time frame and specific deadline for completion. Having a specific end date will keep you from procrastinating.
- WHICH factors will affect the success of your goal? What requirements do you have, and what limitations will you have to deal with? Being prepared for obstacles makes them easier to surmount.

- WHY do you want to reach this goal? The reasons behind your choice of a goal are just as important as the goal itself. Looking at those reasons can often tell you quite a bit about yourself!

SMART Goals are Measurable

A good goal is always measureable. If they can be quantified or measured, we can see our progress relative to the goal. Daily achievement in the form of small steps toward our goal is very motivating. Someone said the more measureable a goal is, the more motivational it will also be.

You should be able to see the progress you are making. This allows you to feel the thrill of each milestone reached, and keeps you on track for completion of your goal. The way you find out if your goal is truly measurable is to ask another set of questions:

> **How much** (weight do I want to lose)?

> **How many** (laps do I want to swim)?

> **How will I know** when the goal is reached?

Charts are a great way for you to track your progress and measure how much of your goal you have achieved.

SMART Goals are Attainable

A good goal is achievable, attainable; it is not so far out in the clouds that it is unrealistic. Your subconscious mind will never help you go for an outlandish goal. If necessary, break down your goals into bite sized, manageable portions. Unrealistic goals tend to discourage people and impede our progress, making us wary of setting any more goals in our lives. This is not to say the goal cannot be challenging, it just needs to be realistic or attainable.

Each goal you reach makes the next one seem more attainable, so as you grow so can your goals! As you stretch to reach the goals you set for yourself, you find out you are capable of more than you ever thought possible. You set goals higher each time as you grow more confident.

Realistic goals not only take into account what you are capable of, but what you are willing to do and what your circumstances permit. A goal can be high and still be realistic. At the same time, what might seem like an easy goal to some might be difficult for others because of factors below the surface.

Setting a high goal may bring a sense of greater motivation, because you can see what a great difference it will make in your life, but at the same time, it can be overwhelming, so break the larger goal down into a series of smaller ones. Your goal is easier to accomplish when it seems realistic to you, and small goals are generally approached with greater confidence of success.

SMART Goals are Relevant

Relevant goals address the *why* question. How is your goal important to you and *why*? When you have a strong enough *why* you tend to find the *how to*. You may need to think about what immediate and long term benefits will come if you reach your goal.

There are workshops that are designed just to help you find your *why*. Why is your goal relevant to you? Are you trying to fulfill someone else's goal for your life? As was pointed out earlier, *The reasons behind your choice of a goal are just as important as the goal itself.* When the going gets tough or you don't think you are making enough progress, reviewing your *why* can get you over the hurdle. It may be helpful to have a printed statement of your goal, motivational posters or pictures of your desired outcomes in places that you will frequently see them.

SMART Goals are Timely

A goal without a due date is just a dream. If you don't have a time frame for the reaching of your goal, you have no real impetus. *Someday* is not an acceptable deadline. Setting a date for the completion of your goal can put you in motion mentally and sets the pace for a steady race to the finish.

Smart goal setting takes into account all of the guidelines above, and helps you develop a right state of mind and a game plan for getting things done. Is your goal a SMART one?

LIVING THE PLAN

What has been your experience with goals? Can you see how the steps in this chapter can help you achieve your desired outcomes?

Begin to write out your goals for this year. Brainstorm what you would like to see happen in your life and then make the steps to get you there. Use the principles in this chapter to write SMART goals. Share your written goals with some trusted friends and regularly review your goals.

21.

AFFIRMATIONS

"Bind them around your neck,
write them on the tablet of your heart."
Proverbs 3:3

An affirmation is basically a statement that describes a desired situation or outcome and is repeated often enough to implant the assertion into the subconscious mind. In order for affirmations to be successful, they need to be repeated with attention, conviction, and commitment.

Everything you say to yourself is an affirmation. How you talk to others reveals your inner dialogue and the affirmations that you have chosen. You are constantly talking in your mind and acting on the beliefs and truisms that make up your convictions. Making new, positive and proactive affirmations has the ability to transform your thinking and your life.

You can program your mind, and then your brain go about helping you live and view the world in the belief structure, or world view, that you believe is true. Of course your chosen worldview may be, and probably is, a bit skewed, but it is very real for you. (Explore the difference between reality and truth in chapter 7.) This is why it is vitally important for you to be proactive and positive about how you speak to yourself.

I have a friend who did not have a very pleasant upbringing. He is constantly berating himself (and others). He not only puts himself down, but he predicts that he will fail at something before he even begins. Talk about self-fulfilling prophecy. This man's self talk is probably very negative and based on a self-concept that was developed over the years of his early negative upbringing. How he thinks about himself is projected into the world in a sort of "rose colored glasses" (only his aren't rosy). You can easily see how by changing his thinking, this man could change his life, but he has apparently never challenged the paradigms in his mind, or maybe even wondered how those got there in the first place.

Affirmations are not just positive thinking. You can try to believe something is true when you know it is not, but your mind will not put up with that for long. Positive thinking is also based on a potentially unrealistic performance by yourself and others. Positive thinking has been compared to pulling yourself up by your own bootstraps; in other words, it just can't be done successfully. Putting a positive spin on something may help for the short term, but it is not a long-term solution.

Affirmations, on the other hand, are realistic and long term. It is much like changing the operating system in a computer. Once you have reprogrammed the computer, it will continue to function along the new programming lines because the old system is no longer valid.

Why Affirmations Work

When you repeatedly state a truism, which you firmly believe, you are imprinting on your brain the specific belief. This idea is forced down into your subconscious thinking and is assimilated into your other beliefs. Your mind likes unity and clarity. Your brain is hardwired to accept what you believe is true and to reject competing ideologies. Your mind will throw out or dismiss ideas that you believe are untrue.

Incidentally, this is why positive thinking does not always work: you may be trying to tell your mind to believe something that is quite unbelievable. **A good affirmation is believable to your subconscious and attainable.** Your mind goes to work constantly filtering out information that is of no use to you and calling your attention to things that bring you closer to your perceived reality. When you get your subconscious on board you supercharge your thinking.

Have you ever had the experience of buying a car and then seeing more and more of your type of car on the road? When this happens, your mind is calling your attention to what was already there (the same other cars), but now it is seeing this information as important to you. It is filtering and processing the information based on your new input. Putting this tool to work for you is what affirmations are all about and why they work so well when done properly.

When a new affirmation is planted and takes root in your subconscious, your mind will challenge any other assumption based on the old programming. Dysfunctional ideas will be replaced and new data will be assimilated. There may be a period of introspection as new ideas supplant the old ones.

Affirmations work because they actually reprogram your old thought patterns and begin to change the way you feel, think and act on things. Older, dysfunctional beliefs are replaced with new positive convictions and your life changes externally for the better. Most models for change making incorporate positive affirmations in some form or another.

How to Create Powerful Affirmations

Let's look at how to create powerful affirmations. Assuming you have written out your goals and know what you want to be or do, you can begin to craft affirmations that will help you achieve your written goals. Let's take, for example, the idea that you have made it a goal to be debt free. You have written down your motivation for this choice and lifestyle and you have a deadline you are shooting for. You wrote a SMART goal for becoming debt free. Your affirmation needs to be written in the positive voice, not the negative voice or what you don't want.

I shared earlier that my daughter, Amanda, once said to me, "Debt free is the way to be." That is a very positive affirmation and truism. Notice how much more powerful that statement is than, "I don't want to live with debt anymore." **An affirmation is a verbal and written reminder of what you want, not what you don't want**.

Notice also that you should write your affirmations in a present tense voice. You write affirmations for what you are currently doing. In the debt free example, another positive affirmation could be, "I am living a debt free lifestyle." Your subconscious mind can believe that and will help you during the day to make the right choices. Imagine you are in the store and a large screen TV is on sale. You have wanted a large screen TV but you would have to put it on credit. If you are seriously imprinting your affirmations, your subconscious will tell your conscious brain that you are committed to living a debt free lifestyle and it may suggest that you reward yourself when you are debt free, by purchasing the TV with cash.

Affirmations are written clearly and vividly. The more clear and concise the better the affirmation. It is like that example of purchasing a new car, where your mind seeks out that car for you, out of all the cars on the road. I heard a friend say once, "I used to think I was the only one who had a red Mustang, now I see them all over the place!" Good affirmations are written so that your mind searches out what you want and helps you make the right choice.

Your affirmations must be believable and achievable. You can't tell yourself that you are going to swim to Hawaii or something equally unbelievable. Your mind will reject that idea very quickly. So, write affirmations that are believable and achievable.

When possible, write the affirmations with a view to support other beliefs and choices you have. Your mind is an organic living thing, like trees, and it is integrated and holistic. One idea relates to many more on your thinking "tree." You might say something like: "I live in the present. Today I am choosing to have my best day ever."

I have included some sample affirmations in the appendix at the end of this book. Use the samples to write your own powerful affirmations. God has given you capacity for imagination, so try to vividly imagine, or frame, a picture in your mind's eye. Then, write a clear, achievable, believable, present tense affirmation.

How to Use Your Affirmations

Now that you have written your positive affirmations, you need to review them often. When I was a minister at the Church of the Open Door in downtown Los Angeles, I had a long bus ride to and from my home in Whittier. This was a time when I became aware that I needed some major changes in my life. I had written out a number of positive affirmations and kept them in my wallet. Every day when I rode the bus to and from L.A., I would prayerfully review my affirmations, allowing them to sink into my heart and life. I would ask God for help in making positive change in my thinking and behaviors. I can say with conviction that this period in my life was the most powerful and life transforming that I ever experienced.

There were some important things that contributed to the success of these affirmations at that time in my life:

- Write your affirmations down
- Review these affirmations often and regularly
- Choose a time when you are relaxed, and virtually alone
- Recite them aloud, when appropriate
- Pray and ask God for the power to change

In addition to these things, in order to implant the new affirmations it is important that you repeat your affirmations with passion, conviction and resolve. The subconscious takes notice when you are emotionally charged. You are really trying to convince your subconscious mind that you mean what you say. If you repeat your affirmations with a weak voice or without conviction you won't even convince yourself!

Some people like to repeat their affirmations in the morning when getting ready for the day. They speak them out loud in front of the bathroom mirror when they are looking themselves in the eye. The mirror can help you see eye-to-eye with yourself. And you can see in your expressions, face and body language that you are serious and mean business. As you look yourself straight in the eye there is little room for misdirection or telling yourself a lie.

Some people find it helpful to have some other tools to aid their transformation process. One of my friends asked me to record his affirmations, so he could hear his affirmations spoken aloud from a trusted friend. This helped him believe the affirmations he wrote, since he valued my opinion. This also gave him some accountability for the items on which he was working. Some people make a recording of their affirmations and listen to them when they go to sleep at night or when they have an available moment. Take the opportunity to listen and repeat your affirmations whenever possible.

Other people put up motivational posters or pictures of what they are trying to accomplish. Making up small cards and placing them around your home and office as reminders could also be useful.

What absolutely does not work is saying your affirmations consistently and passionately and then choosing to continue to make poor choices during the day. You must not only change your attitude but also your actions. There is a direct correlation between our actions and our attitudes and it works both ways. If in doubt, just begin smiling and see what that does to your attitude.

LIVING THE PLAN

Based on your own goals and desire to live today as the best day of your life, look at the affirmations at the back of the book. Begin to make up your own list of powerful affirmations.

Find a place and time where you can repeat your affirmations. Take some of the suggestions in this chapter and incorporate them into your plan for incorporating your affirmations.

22.

LOOKING OUT FOR NUMBER 2

"Do not merely look out for your own personal interests, but also the interests of others."
Philippians 2:4

Robert Ringer made a ton of money with his self published book, "Looking out for number one." He wrote it in 1978, and it became a best seller. The premise of the book is of course, the motivational power of self-interest. He went on to write other books including another best seller entitled, "Winning through Intimidation." I'm thinking Mr. Ringer places a lot of value on self-interest and winning at all costs. He has continued to write other books espousing his beliefs in looking out for your own self-interest.

What kind of society would you have if everyone followed Mr. Ringer's philosophy? Is life really all about you? Unfortunately, the more secularized the United States becomes as a nation (and I am speaking from the vantage point of being an American citizen), the more I am tempted by and see others enticed by the "me" philosophy. Personalized computers, having it my way, iPhone, iPod, iEverything contribute to the idea that I take first place in everything.

Self preservation is normal and natural and, in one sense, you do need to look out for yourself. If you don't take care of yourselves, setting appropriate boundaries, you won't be able to help others. It's the idea of, "In the unlikely event of a loss of cabin pressure...place your mask on, first, then assist others."

Self-preservation, however, can be taken to an extreme. Some people have narcissistic tendencies where they do not even recognize the rights of others. They are stuck in the preschooler mentality whereby, "The world is me." They believe that the world actually does revolve around them.

Unfortunately, a person wrapped up in themselves makes a very small package. Some call people who do not recognize the rights of others selfish people. Selfish people are not expansive; they do not give of their time or wealth to help others. They truly are a small package, and while they may think they are God's gift to the world they really are more of a hindrance.

The roots of selfishness are often found in the early imprinting of childhood. These self-absorbed people may have been deprived as a child of basic necessities; they may not have been unconditionally loved by their parents, or their parents might have not disciplined them properly. Children need to be taught the value of ownership before they learn the value of sharing. Sometimes, parents force their child to share when the child has not learned how to possess material things. Selflessness is a higher self-concept and it needs to be built on a strong foundation of personhood. In many ways I fear for the self-absorbed, pampered and spoiled young people that are on the scene today. They are not "growing up." Instead, they seem to be growing inward and cut off from meaningful relationships.

In our current society, and in most every societal group, altruism is to be preferred over selfishness. Society is actually built on altruism, the ability to look out for your own interests while using your power and influence to help others. Where do people learn this concept? Parents are responsible for training children. Children who get the philosophy of a dog eat dog mentality and the idea to look out only for number one can probably trace this back to their parents.

Children learn altruism by their parents; what is taught as well as what is caught. The words must match the actions. There are four levels of altruistic motivation and a child must matriculate through them to become an unselfish person:

At one level we do something because it is good for me. Self-perseveration falls in this section of motivation. Then we learn to do something because it is good for everyone involved, as we recognize the importance and value of others. The third level is doing something because it is good for the other person, even if it has negative results for me. The fourth and final stage is doing something because it is right. This is the section of motivation moral development comes from.

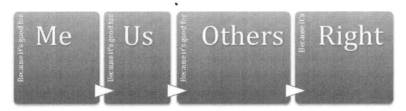

In order to experience the best day ever, you must recognize the importance of self-care, but also look out for the interests of others. You can enrich and empower other people to be and act their best, and this can add value to your life and to our society.

Today can be the best day of your life, even if you are not spending the whole day on the beach tanning yourself. I had a friend who said, "The worst day fishing beats the best day working." I feel sorry for this mindset. Whether you are fishing or you are working, you can have the best day of your life if you decide to make it so. It is really not about you, but what you do with what you have been given. Are you going to live selfishly, only looking out for number one or are you going to enrich the lives of others? It is your choice.

LIVING THE PLAN

Do something today to enrich others, a random act of kindness, an anonymous deed, a kind word or a card of encouragement sent to someone...

Think of an out of the box way that you can overcome selfishness and empower someone else with your life or wealth.

Who really is number one? Colossians 1:18 states: "That in all things, He might be preeminent." How does placing God as number one in your life change your priorities?

23.

UNCONDITIONAL LOVE

"Love is patient, love is kind, it is not rude it does not boast."
I Corinthians 13:4

In order to make today the very best day of your life, you will need to put on unconditional love. Everyone wants to be loved. Loving some people in your life is easy. Loving others, who are by their actions unlovely, or demonstrating unconditional love to random people you meet is almost unthinkable for many people. I watch people who are engaged in road rage or are in public and berating others, and wonder what their lives are like.

Yet, today, in order for your life to be lived to the fullest, it must be lived in the context of unconditional love. There are many conceptions and ideas about love floating around. You may be guilty of believing something to be true that is not true about love, generally, and unconditional love, specifically.

Most of us have been taught to love those who love us. Love is also unpacked as a feeling. Much of what we think of love is actually infatuation. Sexual lust, desire for companionship, wanting to feel wanted are feelings masquerading as love. True love is not a feeling but a commitment. Love is a decision on your part. Think of love in this way: "**Love seeks the highest and greatest good for the other person**."

Love, is not about you, what others do for you, how others make you feel or anything like that. Love is your decision to seek the highest and best for others. With this idea, can you see that love is your responsibility? You are empowered to love others as you choose. Love is empowering.

When you consciously choose to seek the highest and greatest good for another person, you are demonstrating love. This type of love is not self-seeking. Don't love others for what you can get in return; love is not manipulative or coercive.

The miser, the lonely person, who has shut themselves up in a tight cocoon of themselves is not a lifestyle to be envied or emulated. (Like we saw in the last chapter: A person wrapped up in themselves makes a pretty small and pathetic package.) Compare and contrast this person to the one who loves, who gives, who is interested in the wellbeing of others. That person is growing and expanding. They are the type of person people want as a friend.

Some people demonstrate kindness as a way to get what they want from you. If you don't give them what they want they turn on you and become very toxic. If you would like a refresher course, look back on the chapter about boundaries!

Someone said the opposite of love is simply ignoring someone. I think most people realize that the opposite of love is hatred. Expending emotional energy or hate is so unproductive. I have never understood racial hatred. My parents raised us four kids to see the individual behind the skin color. When I was older and traveling in Asia, Africa, South America and elsewhere, I witnessed racial hatred and tremendous animosity like I had never seen before. It is grossly unfair to link people together because of ethnicity, religion or any other singular idea. Each person is unique and very special. At the very least, we should have compassion for all people, even those seeking to destroy us. My wife and I witnessed so much hate and aggression on one trip when we went to Egypt, Jordan, Israel and Palestine.

But the people of Burma showed me another way. The Myanmar Christians are a minority in their Buddhist country. They have been systematically raped, tortured and killed. The atrocities thrown on these gentle people are unspeakable. Yet in my time with the Northern Tribe of Kachin people, they showed me that they were praying for the army that has been sent by the government to destroy them. They are willing to forgive and live in peace if at all possible. Unfortunately, there is no end in sight. Villages are burned and their fields are land-mined by the government. Children, animals or those going back into the village to scavenge or forage are often killed by land mines or maimed for life. But, I have seen in these people a love that is very compelling and amazing. They are truly living one day at a time, making the most out of every day. Hopefully, one day the world community will put pressure on the government of Myanmar to bring much needed peace to the area. For now we pray for them and remarkably, they are praying for us!

In life we will be misunderstood. Our motives will be questioned and people will despise us for the most ridiculous reasons. Even though some people will hate us, this is no reason to hate them back, or return evil for evil. We need to be above this kind of tit for tat emotionalism. We must not let small minded or emotionally stunted people spoil our joy and steal our happiness.

In order to make today the best day of your life, you must be loving person, the kind of love that is unconditional, the kind of love that Christ showed. It is an historic proven fact that Jesus of Nazareth died on a cross. We know from the Bible and other texts that He came to die for the sins of all people and to give His life as a ransom. Here is love, unconditional and free. When you have been touched by this kind of altruistic love you are more likely to give this special kind of love to others. This is the type of love that makes today the best day of your life.

LIVING THE PLAN

Have you ever experienced unconditional love? When?

Can you make a list of all the people who have hurt you and hated you and forgive them, genuinely offering unconditional love if you ever meet them again?

How can you show love to people in your life?

24.

THANKFULNESS

"Give thanks in all circumstances."
I Thessalonians 5:18

Time after time the Bible tells us to rejoice and be thankful in all circumstances. Not all circumstances are good, but with the good, we also accept the not so good. We are never to be "under the circumstances." In spite of our current situation, if it is negative, we can still be above it reframing the experience and not allowing it to sap our joy.

I remember the first time I heard a funny expression of this truth. I had asked an old timer friend of mine how he was doing. He said that it was going to be a good day because he woke up on the right side of the grass. Maybe you have heard that before, I still get a smile when I hear it. Hopefully our days are more than just about waking up on the right side of the grass, but even in the little things we can rejoice and be thankful.

Today there seems to be a spirit of entitlement that is very pervasive. Instead of people experiencing their best day ever, many are angry with life and mad at God. These people may feel like the victim and that they deserve all the happiness life can give. They may feel they have been given a raw deal and end up negative and bitter. This bitterness brings on more bitterness and negativity.

The United States of America is one of the few countries in the world that commemorates a day of Thanksgiving. Our founders realized how blessed they were. I look back on their poverty and sickness and wonder how they could ever have been thankful. I am sure they would look at us today with all we have and wonder how we could ever be ungrateful. We have so much as a nation to be grateful for, but as our society grows increasingly secular, we are less and less grateful to a Sovereign God who gives us all we need and in Whom we can trust. We have come to think we have done all this by ourselves and without the mighty hand of God guiding our country. We are proud of our accomplishments and pride is the opposite of thankfulness. It is ingratitude, the "I did it myself " mentality.

Thankfulness brings more good things into our lives than does ingratitude. There was a young man in Los Angeles, near where my wife and I lived, who always wanted to borrow my tools to work on his car. I had no problem letting him use the tools, but they came back in such a mess that I had to wipe grease, grime and sand off the entire toolbox and every tool and socket. I mentioned to him that I had to clean the tools and that I had anticipated that he bring would them back in the same condition he found them. He did not respect my desire or my tools and the third time he asked to use them, I declined. I told him I could no longer trust him with my tools and that I felt he took advantage me since I had to clean them off after each time he used them. His ingratitude cost him the use of my tools and sadly he did not learn the lesson of gratitude in other areas of his life as well. His attitude toward others became his legacy and it was not pretty.

When you are genuinely appreciative for the smallest things in life you may seem to attract larger blessings. If you gave two children a piece of candy and one turns away without saying thank you, you may wonder if you made a mistake. However, if one of the children turns around and is genuinely grateful, you naturally want to give the thankful child more candy. Our universe seems to operate on this principle: The more we have an attitude of gratitude, the more good can come into our lives and the more we become grateful. It is an upward spiral.

I'm not talking about a pseudo thankfulness that tries to repay a service done or a gift given. My wife and I saw this when we lived in Japan. Asian culture almost demands that good will be repaid, usually in the form of a gift. Then that gift must be recognized and repaid and this is an increasingly larger and larger gift exchange. We saw people who had whole closets full of gifts (presumably that they were given), for when they had to repay someone's kindness. This becomes a spirit of obligation not genuine thankfulness. "Regifting" has become a large part of western society, too, perhaps because of the influence of Asian culture but more likely because we are becoming a people who are less thankful for what we are given.

If the object given is not something we can use, we still can honor the giver through our attitude. In our family my wife and I taught our kids a little saying that became a mantra: "We are thankful for what we are given." We felt it is so important that children learn early an attitude of gratitude.

In order to make today the best day of your life, it will be essential that you are thankful for all the things that come into your life. Obviously, not all things are positive and they may not seem for the moment to be a blessing, but faith the day, believing that God has a higher plan and purpose for your life and that these experiences, especially the difficult ones, are for your development and refinement.

You may be going through something very difficult right now, the loss of a loved one or a medical condition or some other calamity. You have been given the authority to place those things in the loving hands of Jesus. He said, "Cast all your care upon me." His hands are large enough to handle even your greatest challenges. Allow Him to carry the burdens as you walk in the unconditional love, grace, forgiveness and thankfulness. Commit to making today the very best day of your life.

LIVING THE PLAN

Write a list of all the things for which you are thankful. Refer to it in a month and add to it as you remember more items.

Write down all the things for which you could complain; all the negative situations, circumstances, and people. Then, reframe these items as positive influences in your life.

Seek to develop an attitude of gratitude in all things. Help others in your sphere of influence also be thankful. Demonstrate your heart of thankfulness and model it for others.

APPENDIX I

PROVERBS & DAILY AFFIRMATIONS

A proverb is a nugget of truth, a truism. Much of what we believe can be stated in proverbs or wise sayings such as; "Debt free is the way to be." Proverbs are concise statements and are similar to the affirmations we will be developing. Here are some basic commitments:

1. Rewrite the affirmations in your own voice. Include powerful action words that will make an impact on your subconscious.

2. Regularly review your list of affirmations, committing them to memory.

3. Keep proverbs and your affirmations in front of you. Use 3 X 5 cards, voice recordings or posters. If they are in your sight they will be in your mind.

4. Review, review and review.

APPENDIX II

SAMPLE AFFIRMATIONS

I choose to make today the best day of my life.

I consider this day to be a gift from God and I will show my appreciation by living this day to the fullest and best for His glory.

I look for the positive, the highest, the good and the best in every situation I encounter today.

I live today, fully alive, experiencing each moment in positive anticipation.

I live just for today, not holding back- full throttle.

I live with eager anticipation rather than preconceived expectations.

I let go of all past transgressions, hurt and pain. I know the freedom of forgiveness and the healing power of love.

I savor, not squander each moment that I am alive today.

I live in the moment.

I am today, the person I have always wanted to become.

I count my blessings today, not my "things."

I live today with no regrets.

I do it today.

I choose to be happy, at peace and content today regardless of my circumstances.

I live with no thought of self imposed limitations.

I seriously listen to the only expert on my life: me!

I draw and maintain boundaries for dysfunctional or toxic people in my life.

I am aware of the difference between perceived reality and truth and I seek truth.

I fill my mind and heart with positive affirmations and do not listen to voices (including my own inner voice) that demeans, puts down or seeks to derail and destroy my best day ever.

I not only look out for my interests but also the legitimate needs and interests of others.

I live this day with humility and grace.

I exhibit, to everyone I meet, the attitude, aptitude and attribute, of unconditional love and acceptance.

I treasure my relationships in this best day of my life.

I live today with an attitude of gratitude, with thankfulness and joy in my heart.

I review my life's goals regularly and commit to memory my positive, daily affirmations.

APPENDIX III

MY BUCKET LIST

God is a God of Place. He is intimately concerned with places. In the letters to the Seven Churches of Revelation, God says, "I know where you live." God created all the places in the world.

One of the blessings of being as old as I am, is having a lot of experience with places. I have lived and worked in many places. As I look over my life, I have been very blessed. I have had the great honor and privilege to stand in, visit and see some of the most remarkable and amazing places in the world. There is a Hank Snow song that you may be familiar with called, "I've been everywhere." I feel I have just about been everywhere. I truly have been blessed with a remarkable life and the opportunity to visit many wonderful places.

I would like to share a few of those places with you. You might have been to these places as well, and you may have been to many more historic and significant places than I have been. But I want to take you on a quick tour and then to the place where I believe is the most important place in the entire world.

In no particular order, here are a few of the places I have been privileged to visit:

I have climbed to the top of Mt. Fuji, and, while in Japan, went inside the Buddha of Kamakura. They no longer let visitors into the structure. I was in the Dragon Hall in Nara and stood on the top of the Tokyo tower.

I have been in the Gateway Arch in St Louis, Missouri as it gently sways; I have stood at the Lincoln Memorial, and was in the room where Lincoln died, across the street from Ford's theatre.

I have been in the White House. I have been at Versailles standing in the hall of mirrors, where the treaty of Versailles was signed ending the war.

I have stood on the deck of the USS Missouri where Douglass McArthur accepted the Japanese surrender after World War II. I have been aboard the Queen Mary, and sat at the helm of our most modern nuclear aircraft carrier, as she was in port next to the Kitty Hawk. I have floated on the Mississippi on a river boat, and canoed on the Yukon River in Alaska.

I have stood atop the ancient Mayan ruin of Altun Ha where the famous jade skull was found. I have stood in the rock fortress of Petra and explored Masada. I've climbed on the great Pyramid of Giza.

I have climbed the Eiffel tower and the Arch de Triomphe; I have been to the Louvre and seen Mona Lisa.

I have been to the Brandenburg gate, the Berlin Wall and Checkpoint Charlie.

I have seen the mummy of King Tut and marveled at the Dead Sea Scrolls.

Susan and I have ridden camels in the Egyptian desert, traveled on the bullet train in Japan (they are very fast), and been on the

<u>first</u> Air Force One, and the SST.

We have floated in the dead sea, baptized people in the Jordan river and stood on the steps of Herod's Temple in Jerusalem, where Peter preached on the day of Pentecost.

I have stood at Lindberg's grave in Maui and I have hiked the Grand Canyon.

I've walked into Edison's laboratory where he invented the light bulb. I have been in the Wright Brother's Bicycle shop and the boyhood homes of Daniel Webster and Robert Louis Stevenson.

I have been to Ludwig's castle in Germany, twice, and stood on the Prime Meridian in Greenwich, England. I have touched the Titanic and a rock from the moon.

I could go on for about another half hour or so, telling you about the places I've been privileged to see and the things I have been fortunate enough to do. But when it comes right down to it, I have to ask myself, **where is the most significant place in the entire world where I have been?** The most important in the terms of human history. Stonehenge? Mt. Sinai? Our nation's capitol, or Independence Hall, where the Declaration of Independence was signed? Was it a lavish palace or the throne room of a king?

No, I have been so fortunate in my life as to have been in the most important room in all of human history. It is the most significant place in the entire universe. I would trade all of my world travels and all of my experiences to spend another 15 minutes in this place.

This place was not the tower of London, where I saw the crown jewels of England. It was not the Denver Mint, where I was in a room with a million dollars of gold. It was not in the Rembrandt Room of the Musee d'Orsay, where I was surrounded by priceless familiar paintings of the master artist.

No, the room I am referring to is virtually empty. It is a room, more like a cave, carved out of a hill known as Golgotha, the place of the skull, Calvary. For 2000 years, this little hole in the rock has been preserved throughout some of the most intense fighting and wars of the last two millennia. A garden tomb. An empty garden tomb. I am convinced that this is the room and this is the place where my Lord Jesus Christ was placed for the better part of three nights and days and, on Easter morning, rose triumphantly over sin and death, shattering the darkness and bringing eternal life and light to all people.

Founders of religions of this world are dead. None of them have even pretended to rise from the dead. You can visit their graves all over the world. They are dead.

Only Jesus Christ has risen from the grave to take His rightful place as Lord of Lords and King of Kings. And, the Good News just keeps getting better. Not only is the way for us to have eternal life opened by the shed blood and resurrections of Christ, but He has promised to come again. How do we know His resurrection is true? The way we know it is true is because the Bible says it is so. We have it on God's word, and then further testified by many people through many generations that it was as the Holy Spirit recorded it. The stone was rolled away from the tomb, not so Jesus could get out but so that we could see inside. We could see that Jesus rose from the dead and, after many days, went into heaven to prepare a place for His followers.

Now, I don't know about you, but when Jesus says something, like, He is going to die and be raised again, I would believe Him. You can't keep a God-Man down.

The question becomes, How do you or I know if we are going to get into heaven? Many people will say that they have been mostly good all their lives. If you were to meet St. Peter at the Pearly Gates and he asked, "Why should you be allowed to get into heaven?" What would you answer? That you have been good? How good do you have to be?

Unfortunately, there will *always* be a "Performance Gap" of goodness. It's like swimming from the West Coast of the Continental United States of America to the Hawaiian Islands. Could you swim that? Absolutely no one could make the entire journey. We could get the best athletes, and strongest swimmers, and no one could make the swim.

Like swimming from the mainland to Hawaii, no one is good enough to get to God. No one. We could take Mother Teresa, and Billy Graham, and Nelsen Mandela and still...there is a performance gap, because no one is perfect enough to reach God on their own. The Bible says there is none righteous, no not one (Romans 3:10).

Fortunately, we don't have to reach God on our own. Jesus died for your sin, for your gap. He died in your place so that you would be able to one day say, I do not deserve to enter heaven, but Jesus died in my place. He, the perfect, sinless sacrifice for sins, died and did not stay dead. And, because I am trusting in Him alone for my salvation, I am a child of God's and permitted and welcome in heaven.

If you are without Christ, your life is like swimming to Hawaii without hope of ever reaching your destination. You are not going to make it to heaven, no matter how good you are. You are destined to hell, condemned already, as the Bible says.

There is only one thing that can fill the performance gap. The good news is that it is all about Easter. The empty tomb is a reminder. It is the most significant place on the planet. It is a place that shouts to us, "He is not here, He is risen!"

If this makes sense to you, I would invite you to say a simple prayer in the privacy of your own home. Prayer is simply talking to God. You can use your own words or repeat this short prayer:

> *Dear Jesus, I know I am a sinner. I know I need you in my heart and life. Come into my life today. Make me a new person like you promised. Cleanse my heart from sin, and help me to be the person you would have me be. In the authority of Jesus Name, Amen.*

If you prayed this prayer, I would really like to hear from you. I want to pray for you and encourage you in your faith walk. Please feel free to email me or message me on Facebook. May God richly bless you in this the best day of your life!

APPENDIX IV

INDEX OF PASSAGES REFERENCED

LIVING FULLY IN THE NOW

1. HOW TO MAKE TODAY THE BEST DAY OF YOUR LIFE

This is the day the Lord has made. Let us rejoice and be glad in it. Psalm 118:24

2. ONE DAY AT A TIME

Do not worry about tomorrow, for tomorrow will worry about itself. Each day has enough trouble of its own. Matthew 6:34

Encourage one another daily, while it is still called, 'Today,' so none of you will become hardened by the deceitfulness of sin. Hebrews 3:13

Do not boast about tomorrow, for you do not know what a day may bring. Proverbs 27:1

3. TIME IS RELATIVE

There is a season for everything under heaven, a time... Ecclesiastes 3:1

4. LESSONS FROM A GRAVEYARD

You do not know what your life will be like tomorrow, You are just a vapor that appears for a little while and then vanishes away. James 4:14

5. DO IT TODAY

But encourage one another daily, as long as it is called 'today.' Hebrews 3:13a

6. YOU ARE UNIQUE

For you created my inmost being; you knit me together in my mother's womb. I praise you because I am fearfully and wonderfully made; your works are wonderful, I know that full well. My frame was not hidden from you when I was made in the secret place, when I was woven together in the depths of the earth. Psalm 139: 13-15

7. TRUTH & FREEDOM

You will know the truth and the truth will set you free. John 8:32

Do not store up for yourselves treasures on earth, where moths and vermin destroy, and where thieves break in and steal. But store up for yourselves treasures in heaven, where moths and vermin do not destroy, and where thieves do not break in and steal. For where your treasure is, there your heart will be also. Matthew 6:19-21.

Look, I am coming soon! My reward is with me, and I will give to each person according to what they have done. Revelation 22:12

8. FREEDOM OF FORGIVENESS

Forgive us our debts as we have forgiven our debtors.
Matthew 6:12

9. FREEDOM OF FINANCES

The borrower is slave to the lender. Proverbs 22:7

10. FREEDOM FROM FILTH

Do not be conformed to the world, but be transformed by the renewing of your minds... Romans 12:2a

11. FREEDOM FROM POSSESSIONS

Life does not consist in the abundance of possessions. Jesus Christ in Luke 12:15

12. NO REGRETS

...But one thing I do: forgetting what is behind and straining toward what is ahead, I press on toward the goal... Philippians 3:13

13. WHAT'S THE WORST THAT CAN HAPPEN?

And we know that all things work together for good... Romans 8:28

He [God] makes the sun to shine on the evil and the good and sends rain on the just and the unjust. Matthew 5:45.

14. OUR OWN WORST ENEMY

As a man thinks in his heart, so is he. Proverbs 23:7

You brood of vipers, how can you who are evil say anything good? For out of the overflow of the heart the mouth speaks."
Matthew 12:34

15. SELF-IMPOSED LIMITATIONS

I can do all things through Christ who strengthens me.
Philippians 4:13

16. EXPECTATION VS. EXPECTANCY

Faith is the substance of things hoped for, the evidence of things not seen. Hebrews 11:1

...casting all your anxiety on Him, because He cares for you.
I Peter 5:7 NASB

No, dear brothers and sisters, I have not achieved it, but I focus on this one thing: Forgetting the past and looking forward to what lies ahead, I press on to reach the end of the race and receive the heavenly prize for which God, through Christ Jesus, is calling us. Philippians 3:13-14 NLT

...but they who wait for the LORD shall renew their strength; they shall mount up with wings like eagles; they shall run and not be weary; they shall walk and not faint. Isaiah 40:31 ESV

'Bring the whole tithe into the storehouse, so that there may be food in My house, and test Me now in this,' says the LORD of hosts, 'if I will not open for you the windows of heaven and pour out for you a blessing until it overflows.' Malachi 3:10 NASB

17. TOXIC PEOPLE & WHAT TO DO ABOUT THEM

As much as possible, live in peace with all men. Romans 12:18

18. PERSONAL TRANSFORMATION

Do not be conformed to the world, but be transformed by the renewing of your minds... Romans 12:2a

19. IT'S YOUR CHOICE

Choose for yourselves, this day, whom you will serve...but for me and my house we will serve the Lord. Joshua 24:15

20. GOALS

I know the plans I have for you...to give you a hope and a future. Jeremiah 29:11

21. AFFIRMATIONS

Bind them around your neck, write them on the tablet of your heart. Proverbs 3:3

22. LOOKING OUT FOR NUMBER 2

Do not merely look out for your own personal interests, but also the interests of others. Philippians 2:4

That in all things, He might be preeminent. Colossians 1:18

23. UNCONDITIONAL LOVE

Love is patient, love is kind, it is not rude it does not boast. I Corinthians 13:4

24. THANKFULNESS

Give thanks in all circumstances. I Thessalonians 5:18

ABOUT THE AUTHOR

Dr. Mark von Ehrenkrook has been a university professor, professional counselor / life coach, and pastor. He resides in Puyallup Washington with his wife, Susan. He has three grown children and four grandchildren.

Made in the USA
San Bernardino, CA
25 November 2014